estherpress

Books for Courageous Women

ESTHER PRESS VISION

Publishing diverse voices that encourage and equip women to walk courageously in the light of God's truth for such a time as this.

BIBLICAL STATEMENT OF PURPOSE

"For if you remain silent at this time, relief and deliverance for the Jews will arise from another place, but you and your father's family will perish. And who knows but that you have come to your royal position for such a time as this?"

– Esther 4:14

What people are saying about …

take back your joy

"If you feel discouraged, overwhelmed, confused, or discontent in your circumstances, this book is for you. Nicole writes with vulnerability about her incredible journey through loss, uncertainty, and a surprising diagnosis that would ultimately leave her clinging to the promises of God, more dependent on His grace, and with a passion to encourage others. Her life testifies to His presence in suffering, purpose in pain, and a God who won't let go."

Alisha Illian, author of *Chasing Perfect*,
founder of The Gospel Changes Everything

"Nicole is one of the most extraordinary young women I have ever met. She has overcome so much yet walks in so much wisdom. She has not wasted one thing she has survived. This book is a must-read."

Sheri Rose Shepherd, award-winning author

"Nicole Jacobsmeyer's book is about a real God who is present in our real lives. Things happen to all of us—sometimes hard things. Beautifully and sensitively written, Nicole's practical and insightful book guides us to have faith in a God who can fill our lives with joy—no matter."

Nancie Carmichael, author of *Selah*
and *Surviving One Bad Year*

"Buckle up as Nicole takes us on a journey fueled by the character of God and the hopeful message of the gospel. These pages may smell like smoke because she has been through the fire, and it has refined her. How do we love, serve, or forgive, even amid a life that is more than we can handle? Nicole shows us through story backed by biblical principles. *Take Back Your Joy* is a timely and necessary message for the church."

Rebecca George, host of *Radical Radiance* podcast, author, and speaker

"In a world of painful circumstances, we need the depth and faith of grounded women like Nicole. Reading this book felt as if I had just listened to a lifelong friend pour out her heart and her story of pain, trauma, and triumph—and I was hanging on every word. In today's world and culture, I crave honesty, depth, and biblical soundness. Nicole offers all three—with a sense of humor! She weaves Scripture and stories from the Bible throughout her own story, drawing parallels and lessons from the pages of God's Word to her own life. Nicole's story is worth reading, and her faith will leave you challenged and inspired."

Nancy Ray, host of the *Work and Play* podcast

"Nicole tackles tough topics with biblical truth. Her encouragement is relatable and restorative for rediscovering true joy—God-given joy!"

Sarah Molitor, author, social media influencer

take back your joy

nicole
jacobsmeyer

take back your

fighting for purpose
when life is more
than you can handle

joy

estherpress

Books for Courageous Women
from David C Cook

TAKE BACK YOUR JOY
Published by Esther Press
An Imprint of David C Cook
4050 Lee Vance Drive
Colorado Springs, CO 80918 U.S.A.

Integrity Music Limited, a Division of David C Cook
Brighton, East Sussex BN1 2RE, England

ESTHER PRESS and the EP graphic are trademarks of David C Cook.

The website addresses recommended throughout this book are offered as a
resource to you. These websites are not intended in any way to be or imply an
endorsement on the part of David C Cook, nor do we vouch for their content.

Details in some stories have been changed to protect
the identities of the persons involved.

Bible credits are listed in the back of the book.

Library of Congress Control Number 2022933379
ISBN 978-0-8307-8287-1
eISBN 978-0-8307-8288-8

© 2022 Nicole Jacobsmeyer
Published in association with The Bindery Agency, www.TheBinderyAgency.com.

The Team: Susan McPherson, Stephanie Bennett, Judy Gillispie,
James Hershberger, Angela Messinger, Susan Murdock
Cover Design: James Hershberger
Cover Photo: Getty Images

Printed in the United States of America
First Edition 2022

1 2 3 4 5 6 7 8 9 10

062822

Dedicated to my best friend and husband, Andrew.
Without you this book wouldn't be possible.

And to my four precious and strong kids.
May Christ always be your rock and joy
regardless of what life brings your way.

To the Reader

Thank you so much for picking up this book! I've been praying specifically for you for years. While these pages are filled with hope, encouragement, and Scripture, this book also contains some difficult topics. Life can be so hard sometimes, but let's talk about it and fight for the joy, freedom, and victory that are found only in Christ.

contents

foreword

One of my family's most sacred traditions is looking for sea glass on the Connecticut shoreline. What started as a way of entertaining my two energetic boys in the season of cancellations and closures at the beginning of the pandemic has become one of our favorite pastimes and a tradition we are carrying forward as a family. When I hold the pieces of glass that have been worn down by the salt and sand, their edges rounded and their texture smooth, I wonder if this is exactly what God is doing for us: smoothing out our sharp edges. Sea glass tells the story of the cross. Jesus, broken and crushed, became our greatest treasure. It's a tangible reminder of what God's love has been doing all along: making us into something new.

None of us knows what our particular brand of struggle will be in this life. To be human is to know pain, and there is no cure for the human condition. No, we can't eradicate pain from our lives. But when we encounter suffering, we do get to choose what we do with it. Will we react to the feeling in a way that leaves us struggling with the very pain we were trying to avoid? Or will we let our hurt draw us close to the heart of God—a God who took human form to know and absorb our pain—where we can be transformed? Will we let our struggles shape our hearts and form us into something new? Will we be good stewards of our pain?

I wish I'd had Nicole's truth-filled reminders during my own season of hardship—the same reminders that you will find in these pages. This book encouraged me to trust that we don't need to know what is going to happen in this life; we just need to get to know God. Nicole's words will inspire you to not simply settle for knowing *about* God but rather will move you to *know* God and His Word and to pursue a vibrant relationship with Jesus. And it is here that we find joy that extends beyond the boundaries of our circumstances.

Nicole's candor gave me the permission I craved to speak with honesty about what hurts. And her practical wisdom reminded me that joy is found in celebrating who God is, becoming more like Him, and living right in the center of His will. These pages are a hope-filled anthem that will remind you that "the good life" is a life lived with God right where you are.

Survivors have the most beautiful hearts. Nicole is a survivor. Nicole has been a good steward of her pain and has generously shared her growth with us here, gently showing each of us a new way.

Take your time with Nicole's words. Keep a pen in hand. And savor the gracious gift she has given us in this book. Discover for yourself how pain can help us find the joy and make us into something new.

Nicole Zasowski
Marriage and family therapist and
author of *What If It's Wonderful?*

is this as good as life gets?

Having a stomach virus is downright awful. But do you know what's even worse? When your three little boys have it as well, your nursing newborn is crying because she's hungry, and it's all while you're busy on your hands and knees cleaning up and trying to start the laundry alone in the middle of the night because your husband is working the night shift. That actually happened. Did I do it gracefully and full of joy? Absolutely not. Did I text my husband "GET HOME NOW" in all caps? Yes. Yes, I did.

We've all had those days when we feel like life could not get any crazier or more chaotic. Days when our bodies are aching and our minds are weary. We've also faced days that are excruciatingly painful. Days that leave us debilitated, depressed, or dreaming that Jesus would take us home. You may be in a season of desperation when you've lost your fight, and if so, I pray this book has landed in your hands at just the right time. I've walked through more of those seasons than I would have ever expected. The types of seasons that bring so much turmoil that it feels as if you'll never know how to begin again, let alone fight back with prayer. Days when you would gladly choose a stomach bug over whatever you are facing in the present.

I understand that feeling now and wish I'd understood at a younger age the importance of a biblical foundation. Unfortunately, we don't come to this realization during a fifteen-minute sermon at Wednesday night youth group but through the genuine testing of our faith. It takes actually walking *through* trials to start growing. In my case, it took swimming back to shore with all my strength, only to realize it was God who saved me all along.

Let's back up a little. I was raised in a Christian home grounded in Sunday school felt boards, middle school Bible studies, and high school prayer groups, all while memorizing verses such as Jeremiah 29:11, John 3:16, and Romans 8:28. With all my Bible head knowledge, you'd think I'd have known how to practically live out these truths or apply them to my own life when I walked through hardships years later. Nope. The sum of my problems growing up consisted of braces, zits, and hoping I made the team I was trying out for. Of course, we all had the boy crushes and middle school girl drama as well, but I hadn't experienced anything too horrible.

Since life was seemingly easy, I didn't *have* to work out my faith. As Scripture encourages, "These trials will show that your faith is genuine. It is being tested as fire tests and purifies gold—though your faith is far more precious than mere gold. So when your faith remains strong through many trials, it will bring you much praise and glory and honor on the day when Jesus Christ is revealed to the whole world" (1 Pet. 1:7). Because I hadn't been tested in the fire, I simply was not equipped for what was to come.

As life got more complicated and deeper pains came my way—such as betrayal, loss, sickness, and trauma—I thought I'd done something wrong or that I had this whole "Christianity thing" wrong. I needed to relearn as an adult what it meant to work out my faith—something stronger than the few verses I'd learned at Awana to get me through my darkest days.

Much like daily exercise results in measurable gains, we have to consistently fight for our faith in order to develop our own spiritual strength and endurance. We can't just assume that when devastation hits, a few key verses we learned as children will get us through the trials we face. Good habits such as praying, serving our neighbors, teaching others about God, and reading theologically sound books are all things we can be doing to strengthen our faith.

> **Much like daily exercise results in measurable gains, we have to consistently fight for our faith in order to develop our own spiritual strength and endurance.**

But when it comes down to it, the only way to get through trials with joy is to study God's Word, know His character, and be in relationship with Him. As J. I. Packer said in his book *Knowing God*,

"Once you become aware that the main business that you are here for is to know God, most of life's problems fall into place of their own accord."[1]

From my own experience, I can say that the hardships I suffered initially left me hopeless, frustrated, joyless, and longing for answers. After so much heartache, no amount of self-help or motivational words could save me. I couldn't save myself. I felt as if I'd never be fixed, as if someone had shattered my fragile glass exterior with a mighty hammer, leaving me confused and in pieces. I didn't know which way was up and which way was down.

I read all the right books, sang all the right worship songs, went to counseling, and burned myself out "trying" to pull myself out as I had been instructed. When I didn't find the answers, I started to blaze through life on my own, pretending to be unaffected by anything and numb to any pain that came my way—but numb to all joy too.

Everyone told me, "God will never give you more than you can handle." But the truth is, I was way out of my depth and the trials I faced were debilitating.

I began to believe my life wasn't worth living. I couldn't just pick myself up and force a smile. I couldn't fight back anymore, and I started to question everything.

> *Is this as good as life gets?*
> *Is the Christian life just a series of painful trials?*
> *Why is God allowing so much suffering in my life?*

But with each intense crack I experienced, anger, complaints, selfishness, lack of forgiveness, control, and comparison stole my joy and kept me from living free in the victory I knew God had provided through His Son. Because I misunderstood how intertwined the gospel and my sufferings are, I was kept from believing the truth about God's character and experiencing joy in my worst seasons of life. Not the feelings-based joy, but the fullness-and-closeness-of-Christ-in-our-pain type of joy.

The good news is that we can experience Christ's joy *and* Christ as our joy. Philippians 1:29 says, "You have been given not only the privilege of trusting in Christ but also the privilege of suffering for him." (Read that with *joy* as a synonym for *privilege*.) So we have the joy of trusting *in* Him *and* the joy of suffering *for* Him. The privilege of sharing in Christ's suffering is so countercultural in our world and is truly a lost art.

In the pages to come, we'll ask, How do we even fight for purpose and take back our joy when life is more than we can handle? We cannot rescue ourselves, but there is a fine line in our walk with God when we must pick up our mats and allow Him to do the rest (see John 5:8–9). We are actively pursuing Christ and working out our salvation (see Phil. 2:12), and we need to do our part. We are instructed to "fight the good fight for the true faith. Hold tightly to the eternal life to which God has called you" (1 Tim. 6:12). Yes, we are sinners saved by grace, and Christianity is not a works-based religion. But no transformation happens when we're sitting idle in a corner and focused on ourselves. As that saying attributed to Saint Augustine goes, "God provides the wind; man must raise the sail." We are made new in Christ, and we should walk as those who are redeemed and full of hope and joy, regardless of what comes our way. Yes, way easier said than done.

In each chapter, I'll share my struggles and my testimony of how God helped me overcome, in hopes that you too can still fight for joy when life is more than you can handle—true joy found only in Christ. We'll be starting with what I believe are the two most important ways to maintain joy: by knowing His Word and by believing the truth about God. Everything starts with our understanding of the gospel and having an unshakable foundation.

I pray that when you finish reading, you will see your life through a different lens: one of understanding and grace that points to Jesus. We read this promise in the book of Psalms: "Though you have made me see troubles, many and bitter, you will restore my life again; from the depths of the earth you will again bring me up. You will increase my honor and comfort me once more" (71:20–21 NIV).

I pray this book will be an encouragement to you and light a fire in your soul to keep going and submit to God's beautiful plan for your life. I pray that we will constantly humble ourselves and see Jesus in everything we walk through—good and bad. God is bigger than the trials we face, and He has equipped us with everything we need to take the next step.

Life has knocked some of us down, and we may still be flat on our faces, but it's time to take back our joy. It's only with Christ that we can find hope and purpose. More than that, we can and we will experience lasting joy in knowing Him.

Chapter 1

be grounded in the word

Glow Sticks and the Upper Room

"If you're not praying in tongues, you don't have all of Jesus. Do you want *all* of Him?"

I looked around the dark room and quickly shot my hand in the air along with dozens of other high schoolers. The worship band was loud, kids were lying prostrate on the ground, the staff (most of whom were freshmen in college) were laying hands on kids for healing, and the fog machine was flowing almost as fast as the tears of the girls next to me. Looking back now, it was noisy and distracting, but I thought it must be real because I trusted these people. Plus, I thought being a good Christian meant wanting all that God had for me. I kept my hand raised high.

Since I was one of the "bold" ones, I was whisked away to the upper room. Unlike in the book of Acts, it was actually just the office of the youth group leaders. Regardless, God was going to show up in a big way, and we were told to stay if we wanted this encounter with Him. Because God was moving, we were instructed to call or text our parents and let them know we'd be home late.

With every step that led to the upper room, excitement and nervousness filled me in equal measure. Once we reached the room, we were arranged in a big circle and each student was paired with a college student or leader. We sat cross-legged, close enough to one another that I could hear the whispers of those around me.

My leader spoke to me: "The Spirit is in this place. He is groaning within you and wanting to speak out. Start praying! Believe!"

I started praying aloud, "Lord, I want this! I want to speak in tongues! I believe. Help me. Please give me my own language!"

Nothing was happening. Then I heard the girl next to me start saying something and thought, *Oh no, God's passing over me! What am I doing wrong?*

As I was wondering if this whole thing was working for me, my leader returned and noticed I was still praying in English. She told me to start saying words and combining rhyming sounds. Maybe that would do the trick. "It's different for everyone," she said.

She was very straightforward and came across as insightful and deep, so I tried to follow her instructions. I heeded her suggestion and proceeded to say words such as "mabo, labo, kabo, jabo …"

Just like that, I was speaking in tongues! Or something like that …

Unfortunately, nothing miraculous happened while I practiced the string of words. No one was interpreting what I was saying. I honestly thought that if some random person from another country came into that room, he might understand my words. I was a young, emotional high school girl caught up in the moment. I had faith, but it was an immature faith guided by people in the same boat as me.

I remember telling my mom about my experience. I'm sure she was happy I was up late talking about the Holy Spirit instead of out doing drugs or something equally destructive. But it was so late by the time I got home that we didn't take the time to discuss what the Bible actually says about such things.

Speaking in tongues can be an incredible and miraculous gift from the Lord, but Scripture outlines a certain way for this gift to be used. Of course, I didn't know that at the time. First Corinthians 14 speaks to this, with the clear direction that "God is not a God of disorder but of peace" (v. 33), unlike the atmosphere of the room that night. I believe now that instead of being taught about the different giftings of the Spirit, I was learning to follow my emotions. Emotions can be deceiving, especially when we aren't rooted in God's Word.

As the years went on, I continued to let my emotions guide my walk with the Lord. Whether I was told I needed the next spiritual gift or to worship and pray in a certain way, I quickly became the altar-call girl. Maybe you can relate. I was always raising my hand, walking to the front of the church, asking to be prayed over, or doing the next works-based thing to get closer to Jesus. I probably committed my life to Christ at least a dozen times by the time I was eighteen, just to make sure I was truly saved. I wasn't taught how to be a "disciple," a word whose Latin root means "to learn" or "to grasp."[1] I see now that not knowing God's character or understanding the depth of His Word prevented me from finding true joy and peace.

Looking back on that season of my life, I see I didn't face any major trials that brought me to my knees before the Lord. Not having a desperation for Christ or foundation in Scripture caused me to go through the motions at times instead of asking the hard questions. *What's the end goal here? Do I believe everything in the Bible? Why am I a Christian? Why do we go to church? Why do we save ourselves for marriage? Why submit to Christ?* I loved God so much, but I lacked the answers to why I was living for Him. I was young, after all. But where was the substance? Where was the foundation of my faith?

You may recall the story of Jesus being tempted in the wilderness in Matthew 4. What I find fascinating in this passage is not only the character of Jesus but also the power and authority of God's Word.

Jesus fasted while in the wilderness for forty days and forty nights, becoming hungry and physically weak. Satan first tempted Him by suggesting that if He were really God's Son, He could turn the rocks into bread. While some fresh, warm bread probably sounded delicious to Jesus, He knew that only God could sustain Him. So even though Jesus was exhausted and famished, how did He fight back against Satan? With the Word of God: "People do not live by bread alone, but by every word that comes from the mouth of God" (v. 4).

We go on to read that Satan tried to tempt Jesus again, this time by quoting Scripture himself! He took Jesus to the top of the temple in Jerusalem and suggested that He jump off, using a passage in Psalm 91 to assure Him that angels would save Him. Again, while Jesus probably wanted to throw in the towel with His fast and fly off into the distance, He responded to Satan by quoting Scripture for the second time. Instead of trying to prove how awesome He was or having an "I'll show you!" attitude, Jesus remained firmly secure and declared the truth of God.

Satan then made his last attempt to mess with God's Son. If Jesus wasn't going to give in to His appetite or dishonor God, then maybe he could prevent Him from fulfilling His mission to redeem God's people. The Devil took Jesus up to the peak of a high mountain and said he'd give up all control if Jesus would just bow down and worship him. Unsurprisingly, Jesus reiterated another biblical truth from Deuteronomy, saying, "You must worship the LORD your God and serve only him" (v. 10). Jesus knew His identity. And that was that. The Devil went away after failing in his attempts.

We are called by God to live our lives for Him, to deny ourselves as we suffer with Christ, obey Him, and accomplish the will of the Father (see Mark 8:34–35). The only way to do all those things is to stand on the truth of Scripture when trials and tests come our way. The Matthew passage concludes by saying, "Then the devil went away, and angels came and took care of Jesus" (4:11). Do not be discouraged when you face hard things, because God will not only take care of you when you surrender to Him but will also send help when you need it. Like Jesus, we can rely on God's goodness and faithfulness. When we're trying to understand where our foundation lies, there is no better example than Jesus.

A Firm Foundation

As the pandemic began in 2020, it became apparent that many people were lacking any foundation. Even some Christians were either missing or had a weak grounding in God's Word. Our world was going a million different directions as people rushed to find answers. Morals were being tested, values stripped, sin was running rampant, and it seemed as if our spiritual compass was broken. Unfortunately, with most churches closed for a season, every Christian had to make a choice: stay grounded in the Word, the only unchangeable truth, or let the world set the agenda for our faith.

> **Every Christian had to make a choice: stay grounded in the Word, the only unchangeable truth, or let the world set the agenda for our faith.**

During this time, I noticed how important it was to be examining Scripture verse by verse, actually opening our Bibles and reading them thoroughly. Being a student of the Word was the only thing I could stand on. For years, I considered myself to be God's servant, a follower of Christ. Even a witness. I was good at all those roles, but I realized how the key aspect of becoming a disciple was the most important as our culture tested the Christian faith. As Jesus told His followers, "If you abide in my word, you are truly my disciples, and you will know the truth, and the truth will set you free" (John 8:31–32 ESV). Knowing Scripture needed to be first. The other roles would then flow out of that understanding.

Admittedly, during busy seasons in the past, I found that I was reading the Bible but not studying the Word. I hadn't enjoyed studying in high school or college, and I put studying the Word in the same category. I'm sure I'm not the only one who has felt this way. Reading the Bible can feel stuffy at times (*hello, Leviticus and Numbers*), especially if the stories don't seem relatable and the translation you're using is difficult to understand. My experience growing up was more about optics than discipleship. I was drawn to the miracles, wonders, and feel-good rhetoric of Christianity instead of the obedience and faithfulness that result in a deep relationship with Christ.

But when our world was going through this whirlwind of chaos and difficulty, I wasn't the only one being coerced into the world's beliefs rather than challenged to build a stronger foundation in Christ. I knew others were asking questions such as:

- How do we stand on the Word of God when our culture wants to destroy it?
- With all the division and fear, what does Jesus say about loving people?
- Can we take everything the Bible says at face value?
- If we can't count on people we thought had our best interests at heart, who can we count on?
- Where is God in all of this?

Personally, I wanted to make sure I was standing on solid ground every moment. Was I entertaining unbiblical views of God that were popular with the culture around me, or was I standing on the truth of the gospel?

Going back to the basics of working out my salvation and being a student of the Word brought more joy and consistency to my life than anything else. I recognized how important it was for Christians to have a biblical worldview and the truth it provided. Despite loud voices coming at me from every angle, the Word kept me grounded. As the world presented more problems on what seemed an hourly basis, I remained unchanged, not easily swayed. Studying the Bible helps us see our world through a biblical lens instead of a secular one.

Something I found invaluable was investing in a study Bible. If I wanted to be a student of the Word and prioritize my own relationship with Jesus, I needed to know the Scriptures for myself. Learning how to use commentaries and reading different translations helped me develop a greater understanding of God. I even love going all the way back to the Greek and Hebrew meanings and cross-referencing those with what I'm reading.

I've always asked a lot of questions and compared my beliefs with the Word of God. I've tried to understand the context of Scripture in addition to the words themselves. Over the years, the Word has come alive to me as I've become a student instead of letting my emotions guide. I can honestly relate to Jeremiah when he said, "When I discovered your words, I devoured them. They are my joy and my heart's delight" (Jer. 15:16).

Searching Scripture brought me to a new place of understanding so that when the pandemic came our way, I wasn't lost. The best part was that God met me in my questions throughout and I knew it for myself. My faith wasn't based on what my friends and family believed or what I had been told. It was mine all along.

God's Word Is ...

Trials will come our way; Jesus tells us this in John 16:33. We need to know why we believe what we believe so we can stand on the truth of our faith and remain joyful in all circumstances (see 1 Thess. 5:16). This starts with truly knowing His Word. The Bible is more than just a collection of words; it is the revelation of Christ Himself and what He wants to communicate to the world. Joy and hope will come to our lives as we grow in our understanding of the gospel and the authority of Scripture. It's like a light bulb goes off and we finally see things for what they are. My views on God, the world, myself, His purpose for me, and how I live completely changed with deeper clarity of God's transformative Word.

Several important verses helped me in my journey as I tested the Scriptures. I pray these verses help you understand the validity of the Bible so you can stand on unshakable ground.

- God's Word Is Transformational (2 Cor. 5:17)
Standing on Scripture is powerful and will change us. Through the sanctifying work of Christ, we can be filled, changed, and satisfied.

- God's Word Is Timeless (Matt. 24:35)
His words will never pass away. They are as true today as they were two thousand years ago.

• God's Word Is Unchanging (Deut. 4:2; 12:32)
God demands that His words be unchanged,
because He knows the beautiful weight they hold
in our lives. They are valuable and sacred.

• God's Word Is Inspired (2 Tim. 3:16–17)
If we know and trust the character of God, we can
trust Him when He says Scripture is God-breathed
and will equip us for every good work.

• God's Word Is Powerful (Heb. 4:12)
The Word of God is alive! It exposes sin, helps us
see clearly, and defines our beliefs.

• God's Word Feeds Us (Deut. 8:3)
We don't live by earthly food alone. Our spirits
need the living fuel of God's Word.

• God's Word Bears Fruit (John 15:7–8)
When we live by His words, our lives will pro-
duce fruit! There is no such thing as a fruitless
Christian.

• God's Word Is a Weapon (Eph. 6:17)
Much like when Jesus was tempted in the wilder-
ness, we can fight the schemes of Satan with the
Word of God, which is the sword of the Spirit.

• God's Word Helps Us Endure (Phil. 2:16–18)
Life can be so overwhelming, but when we hold
firmly to Scripture, we can endure and continue to
run this race with joy.

• God's Word Saves Our Souls (James 1:21–25)
When we know the Word of God and do what it
says, it has the power to save our souls. We cling to
His words, not forgetting what we hear.

If I believe God is who He reveals He is in the Bible, then the
Bible is all I need to live a life of godliness. God is 100 percent
trustworthy and holy, and that means His Word is too. It is so com-
forting to know that I can take a deep breath and believe the Bible in
its entirety. We don't have to sift through and take a little of this or
a little of that, cherry-picking verses according to what makes sense
in our finite minds and throwing out the rest.

It can be hard to understand everything God did in the Old
Testament and wrap our minds around every story in the whole
Bible. Think about Jonah in a huge fish, Lazarus walking out of
the tomb, Noah's ark, Jesus feeding the five thousand, or a donkey
talking to Balaam. How in the world? Did these things really happen? The answer is always yes if we trust the God who inspired every
word in the Bible for our edification and instruction.

It's valuable to read all the verses too, not just the ones that make
us feel good. For example, we can't accept that Jesus came to earth
but then throw out the divine virgin birth. Or believe that Jesus died

for us but forget how depraved we are without Him. We can't focus on His love and grace without accepting His justice and how much He despises sin. When we accept the Bible completely, we are able to compare it to what the world is telling us. We can take Scripture at face value and know that everything in it points to the beautiful story of Jesus.

> **There is so much we won't know until we get to heaven, but let's hold tight to the simplicity of the gospel and the treasure of searching for more of Him.**

God's Word may not always make perfect sense because of our limited understanding. There is so much we won't know until we get to heaven, but let's hold tight to the simplicity of the gospel and the treasure of searching for more of Him. I love how Thomas Guthrie put it: "[The Bible] is an armory of heavenly weapons, a laboratory of infallible medicines, a mine of exhaustless wealth.... It is a guidebook for every road; a chart for every sea; a medicine for every malady; a balm for every wound.... Rob us of the Bible, and our sky has lost its sun."[2]

Greater Depth

I remember walking into church one Sunday morning back in high school when the greeters at the door were handing out glow sticks.

Well, this could be fun.

Before I knew it, the lights went off and we began dancing and singing and jumping around. The pastor was sweating, people were standing on their chairs, and we were worshipping freely. It felt like a special and glorious way to worship the Lord. I had never experienced a Sunday morning church service like this, but it was definitely fun in the moment.

I love a good dance party. In fact, my kids and I crank up our music and belt out songs in the kitchen on a weekly basis. But what happens when that mountaintop experience doesn't last? When I handed back the glow sticks and went home that morning, all I had left was an experience and a mini workout session. Was I still worshipping when I left the building?

Ultimately, hype is temporary and never endures like the Word of God.

Sadly, just months after my glow stick experience, it was revealed that the pastor was caught up in sexual immorality and illicit drugs. I share this because when it comes to being disciples, it's all too common to prioritize our feelings and experiences in the church. When our faith is not grounded in Scripture, unbridled emotion can easily lead to deception.

Coming from this church background made me see the trials of the pandemic differently. Thankfully, the chaos of 2020 fostered a desire in me and so many others for something more. I want to cultivate my relationship with Jesus. I want to be fed by God's Word and understand His Scripture daily.

Of course, I still have questions, but I don't sit in them. I pursue them and crave deep answers found in God's Word. I came to a point where I had to either believe the authority of the Bible as my ultimate truth and my daily bread or live a life of convenience and pick out what suited my fancy and stroked my ego.

> # When our faith is not grounded in Scripture, unbridled emotion can easily lead to deception.

It's extremely difficult to humble ourselves and live for Jesus. It means daily surrender, a selfless choice to put our desires to the side. But let's not be fooled into thinking that giving up our lives for God is awful. That's exactly what the Enemy wants us to think—that living for Jesus is just a depressing, un-fun, and sad life. It's in that process of sanctification and searching for Him that we will find wholeness in Christ. When we place our shame, doubts, insecurities, and plans on the altar, God will replace them with joy, strength, and hope. His Word breathes life and purpose into us.

As 2 Corinthians 4:2 says, "We reject all shameful deeds and underhanded methods. We don't try to trick anyone or distort the word of God. We tell the truth before God, and all who are honest know this." The Word of God is pure and honest. There are no tricks or games in knowing His powerful Scripture. Jesus, the Word, became flesh, then died to defeat sin and death for us. God's Word is the gospel and gives us hope of spending eternity with our heavenly Father. We can rejoice in that truth today!

reflections

Take Action

Have you ever been led or overwhelmed by your emotions? If so, how did you switch your focus from an emotional faith to an obedient, Christ-centered relationship? Take some time to open the Bible and fill your mind and heart with God's truth.

Key Verse

"The word of God is alive and powerful. It is sharper than the sharpest two-edged sword, cutting between soul and spirit, between joint and marrow. It exposes our innermost thoughts and desires." (Heb. 4:12)

Closing Prayer

Lord, I come before You now, ready to live out my faith anchored by Your truth. I confess that there have been times when I've let my emotions dictate my path instead of standing firm on the Word. When life is difficult and everything around me is in chaos, may Your Word provide security and hope. Help me to crave Your Word and study it with diligence. I pray that Your words will come alive and that You will use the Bible to speak to me, change me, and be my sustaining bread of life. I desire to worship You in spirit and in truth.

believe the truth about God

Purity Rings and Pets

I have fond memories of my childhood. My parents loved me, I had great friends to Rollerblade and play Barbies with, and I was involved in dozens of sports and activities from the time I was three years old. My parents let me try virtually everything from Girl Scouts to ice skating to soccer to volleyball—you name it, I did it. They also encouraged my creative juices to flow. What started with homemade greeting cards in middle school turned into painting my furniture and even Bible verses on the walls of my bedroom in high school.

Throughout my upbringing, I also had bouts of "pet fever" that my parents graciously accepted. We had a couple of dogs, but I really only loved them as puppies. I remember wanting a bunny so badly as a ten-year-old that I finally convinced my parents it was a great idea. We went to the house of our friend who lived on a farm, and I picked out the cutest bunny—Little Sugar. She was so fun to play with in our front yard, but it wasn't even a few months before (1) I lost interest and (2) I realized I couldn't afford her food and bedding on my meager allowance. So, Sugar went back to the farm.

Then came the birds. I was convinced that a couple of birds in a beautiful white cage hanging from the ceiling by the back door of my room would not only be the perfect addition but would also make me feel so grown up. Unfortunately, a few months later, that ended as well when one of the birds' heads got stuck between its feeder and a bird mirror. My thirteen-year-old heart couldn't handle it. Bye-bye, birdie.

I tried it all: sports, activities, art, and pets. My parents encouraged my God-given qualities and passions as a little girl. They let me figure out my strengths and weaknesses, and I had the best time learning who God made me to be. Which, we now know, is not a pet person.

Although our family moved quite a bit growing up, it was almost as if I had a Christian bubble around me wherever we went. Most of my friends were Christians, and life was simple, fun, and innocent. I was even baptized in a one-piece Minnie Mouse swimsuit in an Oregonian lake when I was in elementary school. I did the right things. Hung out with the right people. Read the Bible. Went to church. Got good grades. Excelled in sports. Proudly wore a purity ring. Had lots of friends. I was joyful—*happy*, rather.

I don't think I truly knew the difference between joy and happiness at the time. Joy is unchanging but happiness is a feeling, something that can change in the moment based on our circumstances. I was operating in happiness. I was a carefree, bubbly person with a zest for life. I loved people, had hope for the future, and thought life was wonderful. Looking back, I understand how fortunate I was to have the upbringing I did.

It was easy to love God in those early years. After all, He was blessing me with so much that I didn't even know there was another side of my faith in Christ yet to be tapped into. The type of faith that keeps going regardless of your circumstances. The type of faith that remains steadfast when everything around you is falling apart. The type of faith that requires you to fight and work hard to develop. I hadn't experienced that yet, and honestly, I was too naive to think my life would ever contain much suffering. In only a few years, I'd realize the depths of pain that life can bring, coupled with the depths of Christ's love.

Real Trials

When we're going through tough times, our friends' and family's first instinct is to try to make us feel better, usually with hugs and encouraging words (although my personal favorite is chocolate chip cookies). However, sometimes words and Scripture aren't enough. Yes, I said that. We can be too deep in our pain to see their truth. When God allows the worst things in our lives—whether it be death, abuse, trauma, pain, broken relationships, infertility, sickness, or other dark devastations—the last thing that feels true is that it all happens for our good and God's glory (see Rom. 8:28; 1 Pet. 1:7). It's hard to hold on to that truth when we're in the middle of suffering or painful trials.

When I was in college, I went through a horrific experience that made me doubt God's love and protection over my life. I hit rock bottom the night I was raped, and it left me wondering how I could recover or trust God again. He claimed to love me and could have stopped this traumatic event, but He didn't. He could have saved me, but He didn't. He is all-powerful and all-knowing, so He could have put someone in my path to help, but He didn't. He could have changed the circumstances, but He didn't. I couldn't understand why God didn't fulfill His promise to protect me.

I went to the book of Psalms: "God is our refuge and strength, always ready to help in times of trouble" (46:1). How could I ever trust God or His Word again? I read this and other verses about God's protection and promises, but the words seemed distant, as if I were reading science fiction or fantasy. I desperately wanted the Bible to ring true in my life and heart, but instead, I felt the opposite.

God hadn't been my refuge that night. Instead, it felt as though He'd forsaken me. He allowed me to be defiled. Why would a loving God, who promised to be my refuge and help in times of trouble, not follow through? Did I do something wrong? Why didn't it feel like He was the loyal God others claimed Him to be throughout the Bible?

I read verse after verse and couldn't find a silver lining. We're often told that God allows difficult things in our lives to help teach us something. But what He allowed in my life was not a lesson for my spiritual growth. Lessons are for when we need a gentle nudge. I was a victim and didn't deserve to be violated. It was not a soft nudge in the right direction but rather a full-on beating straight out of left field for seemingly no purpose.

The truth was that I had little prior experience with trauma and was left confused about who God was. Christian books left me feeling depressed. Worship was confusing. Talking about it made me relive the event, over and over again. Worst of all, my "Christian" counselor was quick to try to medicate and label me. I didn't know how to pull myself out of despair. I didn't know how to feel or act or what to believe anymore. I had difficulty applying what I had learned growing up, and I wasn't prepared for this trial. Not that we're ever prepared for horrible situations, but my foundation had been shaken and I struggled to understand how a loving God would let this happen to me.

The fact that God didn't show up in some way when I needed Him most felt like the biggest betrayal of my life. I felt unloved, unseen, uncared for, unknown, and confused. While all those feelings are valid after a traumatic event, they revealed something deeper. As time went on, I realized I didn't believe that God could actually turn something horrible into something for His glory. I misunderstood the powerful nature of God. Unfortunately, this specific trial robbed me of belief that I could have any joy in the future.

I forgot my place in life and sank under the weight of it all.

Deepening Your Faith

In case no one has told you before, I want you to know that it's okay to question God. It's okay to want to dig deeper in order to understand more of Christ. It's okay to read something in the Bible or hear something from the pulpit and think, *Did that really happen? Is God really like that?* God wants you to search after Him and make His Word your daily bread. As Jeremiah 29:13 says, "If you look for me wholeheartedly, you will find me."

Placing your faith in Christ and following Him doesn't mean smiling amid suffering and never asking questions. No. The opposite of faith is unbelief, and unbelief is the sin. But it's okay to question and wrestle with the Lord on hard topics and things that don't make sense. More than that, this process is *good* because it draws us closer to Him. And that's the goal—to know more about Him and be made more like Him. As long as we are careful and our "hearts are not evil and unbelieving, turning [us] away from the living God" (Heb. 3:12), we can freely ask Him questions.

Placing your faith in Christ and following Him doesn't mean smiling amid suffering and never asking questions.

For instance, when my husband and I have a disagreement or fight, we hash it out and talk through all the details—and we are so much closer afterward. Talking exposes the real insecurities and questions of our hearts. It helps bring to light the actual issues at hand, and when those things are settled in our hearts, it ultimately brings lasting joy.

Questioning is normal. I have cried out to the Lord so many times throughout my life, even yelling out loud, "Help me in my unbelief! Help me understand the reasons for this situation, and help me know more of Your heart, Lord!" We can rest knowing that

God is waiting with open arms for His children to come to Him, regardless of our emotions and whether we feel our best or not.

God always shows up, just maybe not in the way I expect. He doesn't give me all the answers audibly, but He speaks to me through a friend, His Word, or the Spirit in prayer. It's in the stillness of my tears as I humbly come to Him with an open heart that I find the peace and joy I was searching for. But it starts with knowing God. It starts with trusting that He is good and that He loves me. The Ephesians 2 kind of love: "Because of his great love for us, God, who is rich in mercy, made us alive with Christ even when we were dead in transgressions—it is by grace you have been saved" (vv. 4–5 NIV).

That is love. While we were dead in our sins, wretched before Him and destined for hell, God made a way for us by sending His Son as the ultimate sacrifice so that we could be in relationship with Him for eternity.

When we recognize our depravity and need for a Savior, we don't just pray for Jesus to "come into our hearts," but instead, we pray with boldness and repentance that Jesus would take over and do an entire transformative work in our hearts. When I understood that there's nothing good in me, it made the world and my trials look completely different. Everything I had was His, and when Jesus died on the cross, He not only bore my sin but also carried my pain and sorrows. Every trial I would ever go through, Jesus had already taken to the cross: "Surely He has borne our griefs and carried our sorrows" (Isa. 53:4 NKJV).

Understanding the correlation between our pain and being crucified with Christ is so powerful! He carried not only my sin and shame on that cross but my grief and sorrows also. Sickness, death, relational issues, abuse, anything that people do to us, anything that life brings, *and* our personal sin, He bore for you and for me. That doesn't mean I'll have a perfect life with no suffering, but it does help me remember that He is with me no matter what I go through.

Before my terrible experience, I had focused only on the sin that He carried for *me*, which brought me to repentance, but I had failed to grasp that He also bore all the pain that I'd walk through because of the sin in this world. Knowing that He shares in my sufferings allows me to unite with Him in victory and be confident that with Christ I can get through the worst things. He is not a distant God.

> **I had failed to grasp that He also bore all the pain that I'd walk through because of the sin in this world.**

That is the gospel, friends. Clearly, my misunderstanding of the basics of God's character left me in a dark hole of doubt, wondering why I was on this earth and whether He truly was good. That had completely robbed me of any hope or joy.

I desperately wanted to know more of Him for myself. As I searched for Him, Scripture started making more sense, and as I read, I saw glimpses of His character. This previously far-off God was slowly becoming my Comforter, Provider, and loyal Father.

God's Character at Work

Sometimes I feel bad for my husband because he has to live with the intense sense of urgency I feel in almost every situation. Kids are cranky and overtired? I put them all down for naps in record time. If I'm told to schedule an appointment within the next few weeks, I call immediately and schedule it for the next day. When a friend leaves a message asking me to call her back sometime, I do it right then. If I'm asked to do anything, I do it as soon as possible. My email inbox is never full, and I respond to texts when I get them. (The more kids we've had, though, the harder these all get.) But that's just how I am. Gotta get things done! My laid-back husband, on the other hand, is able to prioritize tasks and responsibilities according to what's most important, separating what needs to be done now versus what can wait.

This tendency of mine causes trouble when I bring my strong sense of urgency to things of faith. When I call on the Lord and pray about something, I expect God to act immediately. If He doesn't do what I believe is best or in the timing I want, I easily become frustrated. It sounds so selfish and immature when I put it that way, because we are talking about the God of the universe here. But I find it so hard to let go of my need to get things done quickly and trust that God is operating on a divine timeline.

The Bible is filled with stories that demonstrate God's character and timeline. One of my absolute favorites is found in John 11 because I relate so much to the people and it illustrates Jesus' love and perfect timing. Lazarus and his two sisters, Mary and Martha, were close friends of Jesus. Jesus and His disciples often stayed at their house when they were passing through Bethany doing ministry.

One day, Lazarus became very ill. So ill that Mary and Martha sent a message all the way to Jesus (who was in another town at the time) to let Him know their brother was sick (see v. 3). Mind you, they didn't even ask Jesus to come quickly and heal him, because they probably assumed Jesus would do that since He loved Lazarus.

All Mary and Martha did was state the problem. How many of us do that in our prayer life? We list our problems as "Lord, I am so weary!" or "Lord, my kids are struggling!" We don't ask God for wisdom and grace or specific help because we're stuck in the problem.

What does Scripture tell us Jesus did next?

Jesus stayed in the town where He was for two more days before journeying back to Bethany! (See v. 6.) What? Think about that. Lazarus, Martha, and Mary had chosen to follow Jesus. They knew He was a miracle worker and had healed countless people. Jesus loved Lazarus and his sisters (see v. 5). I'm sure both Mary and Martha expected Jesus to heal their brother right away. These two women must have been furious that the Messiah, who could have healed Lazarus with one word, apparently didn't feel any urgency to return immediately to their home. I imagine they had the same question that many of us have had: "Where were You, Lord?"

But Jesus was acting in the timing of God, not man. The passage goes on to say that Jesus was deeply troubled to hear about the death of Lazarus, and He even wept (see vv. 33–35)! Why would He weep with Mary when He planned to raise Lazarus from the dead just minutes later? Why would Jesus waste tears when He already knew the outcome? I think this demonstrates clearly that God cares about our tears and sorrow. He may choose not to resolve a situation in the way we expect, but He is present in our suffering and pain.

I can imagine how confused Mary and Martha were in the moment. But Jesus didn't merely heal Lazarus. He raised him from the dead to glorify God and showcase His power (see vv. 38–44)! God not only meets us where we are but also uses every situation for our good "so we may learn that He often permits us to pass into profounder darkness, and deeper mysteries of pain, in order that we may prove more perfectly His power."[1] He doesn't rush to get to the next thing, and He is patient with us while we grow to trust Him more.

> ## He may choose not to resolve a situation in the way we expect, but He is present in our suffering and pain.

God is gentle with us as we recognize and remember that He has a bigger and better plan. He will work in ways we could never imagine and redeem things we never thought possible. His love is so deep that He promises to use the best things and worst things in our lives if we submit to Him. He is preparing a place for His children, but while we are on earth, His Spirit—the same Spirit that raised Jesus from the grave—lives in us (see Rom. 8:11).

We have everything we could ever need to get through the worst days in life. No amount of wine, no motivational speaker, no shopping spree, no relaxing bath, no relationship—nothing on earth—can ever match how Jesus Himself shows up in our lives. I'm still learning so much about His character, but one thing I know to be true is that He is not distant, even when we think He is, and He will never turn His back on our pain.

Jesus is with us. He is troubled when His children are upset, and it grieves His heart that there is sin in this world and not everyone chooses Him. But we can be comforted knowing He cares so deeply for us, whether we journey through painful circumstances or are on the mountaintop. Even better, we can have lasting joy with Him, no matter the season, as we hold on to the hope of Christ.

The Flip Side

While we need to understand God and grow in Him daily, we also need to understand His adversary. The Devil is real, and he wants to steal, kill, and destroy those who belong to Christ. Satan isn't worried about those who don't trust Jesus as their Lord and Savior, since they aren't a threat to him.

When we believe Jesus is the only way, there is a large target on our backs! Satan wants us to forget who we are in Christ. He wants us to turn our backs on God and blame Him when bad things happen. He wants us to be entrapped by our sin and shame and misunderstand God's Word and character. Satan wants us to pout, play the victim, doubt, go inward, twist Scripture, think the Bible isn't enough, and lose all hope and joy so that we eventually cave and say no to Jesus. This should ignite a passion in us to live for Jesus and rest in the truth of His character.

Looking back now, I see that God met me in my doubts during this season. At my worst, He patiently allowed me to wrestle with the vastness of His character. While I was questioning and confused, He was there. While I felt alone and betrayed, God was close and already at work to redeem what had been lost.

Moving Forward

There I sat, watching for those pink lines on the pregnancy test. While I was numbed to all pain and experiencing posttraumatic stress and anxiety from the rape, I was also thinking through the rest of my life. What would I do if the test was positive? I couldn't have a baby, not now, not like this. I was still in college with big plans and dreams. But I also knew God would not be surprised by two pink lines.

The Bible says children are a blessing no matter how they come into the world (see Ps. 127:3). I had been physically and emotionally disrespected, but I knew in the back of my mind that the least I could do was honor the miraculous way God creates life by having the baby if I was indeed pregnant. Ending a life wouldn't be justice for what happened to me.

Psalm 139:16 says, "You saw me before I was born. Every day of my life was recorded in your book. Every moment was laid out before a single day had passed." God knows us before we are even formed in our mothers' wombs. Think about that. Before we were even conceived, God saw us.

I could envision both outcomes. I saw my current dreams being dismantled if a baby were to come from this. But I also couldn't let go of the fact that God's plans for me are so much bigger than what I might imagine. If He gave me life and breath, how could I take that away from someone else? Did I really believe I should have the power and right to stop another human being's heartbeat and label it an inconvenience?

Fortunately, the pregnancy test was negative. However, the following weeks were incredibly rough and involved intensive counseling. After the initial physical examination and police reports, I felt as if I were living my worst nightmare. I couldn't see through a thick fog that seemed to constantly envelop me, and this grief and confusion loomed over me for years. My naturally bubbly, energetic, fun, and joyful personality went out the window along with my innocence. I suppressed my trauma and continued with my life.

There was no magic Bible verse or book that pulled me out of the pit. There was no single sermon or event that helped me heal. But looking back, I see that God was strengthening me all along (see Isa. 41:10) by simply being close. I had a sense of His love and presence, knowing that things would be okay and that He was going to get me through one step at a time. While it didn't always *feel* like God helped me in the ways I thought were best, in the long run, He did, and I learned to rely only on Him.

When we walk through the worst seasons of our lives, if we truly know the God we serve, then we know the battle can't overtake us. While our present circumstances might not be pleasant, our future is secure. If we are walking through depression, pain, or other darkness, there is hope. We can have victory and joy now, knowing we are bought by the blood of the Lamb and we will spend eternity with Him.

When God doesn't act in our timing, it doesn't diminish His love for us. It also doesn't make Him lose credibility or impact who He says He is. While it may *feel* like those things are true, they simply aren't. We must have a mature faith to distinguish the truth of who He is from the lies and move forward by embracing the joy and hope of Christ.

Honestly, we are sometimes given more than we can handle to reveal our need for Christ. But one thing that has helped me is reflecting on key character traits of God. Read through the list below. I pray it renews your faith in Him today, bringing you joy and strength to get through whatever trials may come.

- God Is Just (Rom. 12:19)
  God will hold every individual to account on judgment day. He will make all things right.

- God Is Merciful (Ps. 86:15)
  God is full of compassion and mercy for our suffering. He is always willing, ready, and able to walk with us through the worst.

- God Is Peace (Isa. 26:3)
  When we trust in the Lord, He will keep us in perfect peace. Whatever comes our way, good or bad, He provides peace and security.

- God Is All-Knowing (1 John 3:20)
While life constantly throws us curveballs, God is not surprised by anything. He knows what will happen, and He's ready to walk with us through it.

- God Is with Us (Josh. 1:9)
God's Spirit dwells in us. We have nothing to fear.

- God Is Love (Rom. 8:37–39)
No trauma, no person, no death, no government rules, no pain—nothing on this earth—can ever separate us from God's love.

It took time for me to see what God was doing when all seemed lost. It honestly took me years to relearn aspects of God's character for myself while trying to walk in His truth. When we don't know the God we serve, it's hard to view life through an eternal, hope-filled lens.

Now looking back, I see how God doesn't waste a thing, and I've learned that I never have to endure such pain alone again. First Peter 5:10 says, "After you have suffered a little while, he will restore, support, and strengthen you, and he will place you on a firm foundation." God was so gracious to use one of the worst things I'd face to draw me closer to Himself and refine me to become more like His Son. I held on to this incredible promise from God in my darkest times, and I still do when I face unbearable pain.

I pray that we can walk in the abundance of God's character so that when He seems absent, we can rest in this truth: His character always stands the test of time. God is unchanging, holy, always working on our behalf, and full of unending love for us that will carry us through anything we face. That right there should have us rejoicing.

reflections

Take Action

Think of the most difficult season you've weathered and how it impacted your view of God's character. Was your understanding of Him clouded by your trials? Do you see Him more clearly now? Regardless of your circumstances, take some time to refocus on God and His truth.

Key Verse

"In his kindness God called you to share in his eternal glory by means of Christ Jesus. So after you have suffered a little while, he will restore, support, and strengthen you, and he will place you on a firm foundation. All power to him forever! Amen." (1 Pet. 5:10–11)

Closing Prayer

Lord, thank You. Thank You for walking with me through the darkest times in my life. Thank You for being the only sure thing when my world seems to be crashing down around me. Help me to always trust Your character over my own feelings. As I look back on my life, help me see how close You were the whole time. You rescued me and placed me on a secure foundation. Without You I'd still be drowning in the waves. Thank You for turning every horrible situation into an opportunity to learn more about You and become more like You. I surrender my life and trust that You are holding me close, despite the hard things I will face in the future. I trust Your character and know You are the only one I need.

choose forgiveness

Don't Drink the Poison!

I wish I could tell you that joy follows immediately after forgiveness.

I wish I could tell you that it's easy to forgive and move on.

But unfortunately, I'm still learning forgiveness the hard way. Oftentimes the words "I forgive you" don't flow smoothly out of my mouth but instead taste bitter, as the person on the receiving end seems undeserving. While I have seen time and time again that forgiving others releases me from a jail of bitterness, it can be difficult to choose forgiveness when I've been deeply hurt. I'm talking about the deep kind of hurt that cuts straight to the heart, confuses you, or leaves you questioning your purpose.

I've shared that following God wasn't a struggle for me growing up. Obviously, following God is easy when life is good. In high school, I had mostly straight A's and lots of friends. I attended my church youth group, went to a Christian small group for athletes, and was involved in a prayer group. I earned a full athletic scholarship to a college in California and graduated from high school full of excitement for what God had in store for me.

During the first few weeks of college, I quickly discovered that living a bold Christian life in an extremely secular environment wasn't as easy as I'd thought. Over the next eight months, I suffered through verbal, mental, and emotional abuse from my volleyball coach. The ripping apart of my self-esteem led to a series of events, each compounded by the difficulties I faced. What started with academic probation led to coping with the stress by overeating and gaining weight.

Then to top it off, a bad relationship that I thought would fill a void led to my decision to have sex before marriage. I guess the purity culture I grew up in was more about finding the perfect purity ring at a department store and showing it to my friends than about holding a firm identity in Christ and understanding the sanctity of marriage. But that's a story for another time.

While my outward struggles were obvious to some, I hid the deeper internal wounds. These experiences at college stripped away my spiritual defenses, and I started to question God's love and will for my life. Because I felt devalued and used, bitterness and depression took root. I had faced difficulties before, but not true trials like this. The joy I'd known as a younger woman was completely snuffed out, and I didn't even recognize myself.

After my disastrous freshman year, I decided to quit the volleyball team and move back home. While it was the right thing to do, I felt like a complete failure, since it had been my dream to play in college and I'd worked toward that scholarship for years. All the hours dedicated to practice, early-morning tournaments, and long days in the gym felt like wasted time and effort. Now I was walking away. I wanted to build a new life, but I had no idea what I was going to do, because quitting had never been a possibility in my mind. While I looked for a fresh start in a new college and volleyball program, nothing prepared me for what was to come next.

Just when I thought things were looking up, my dad dropped a bomb on our family. The memory is vivid to this day: I was sitting in the living room on our beige couch facing the front door as he told us about his failures and shortcomings. He admitted he was living in sin and shared details of his double life.

This devastating news completely broke me. I went from "We can all get through this" to "I never want to see your face again" in a span of five minutes. Hurt flooded me, and I vowed that my dad's actions were too unforgivable to even pray for healing. My relationship with my dad was over.

He was supposed to be my protector. He was supposed to represent Christ in our home and adore my mom. He was supposed to guide our family and speak with wisdom. He was supposed to live an upright life and be an example to his kids.

Now that was all gone. He had been living a lie.

Two months later, I was raped.

This wave of painful events, one after another in such a short time, rocked my entire view of God and truly left me in the worst place I've ever been. *Broken* doesn't even begin to describe how I felt. My entire identity and beliefs had been shattered, so all that was left of me was dust that scattered in the wind. How was I supposed to handle this pain and heartbreak? My anger and drive for justice caused me to question God. How could I ever trust another man?

How could God expect me to forgive my volleyball coach, my dad, and the rapist for the pain, dysfunction, and confusion they had brought into my life?

As you can imagine, I didn't have any joy, and forgiveness was the last thing on my mind. I thought forgiveness might come years or decades down the road, if ever. *I'll do that later,* I thought.

But I quickly learned that if I wanted healing and joy, I would need to walk in forgiveness.

No matter how it seems in the moment, darkness will not win and the Enemy has nothing on God.

A few days after my dad's confession, he came upstairs to talk to me. Before he could say a single word, I looked him straight in the eyes and said, "You will never walk me down the aisle or be involved in my life."

I may also have said some other choice words I won't mention here, but when someone hurts me, my inclination is to take matters into my own hands. I was trying to fend for myself, and so, in turn, I wanted to punish my dad, send the man who raped me to jail, and expose my volleyball coach. I wanted them to pay for their mistakes because I wasn't seeing God act in a timely fashion.

Why did I feel this need to be the judge? I wasn't trusting God, and I had forgotten His instruction: "Do not take revenge, my dear friends, but leave room for God's wrath, for it is written: 'It is mine to avenge; I will repay,' says the Lord" (Rom. 12:19 NIV). I wasn't doing my part in forgiving and leaving the judgment and healing to God.

If we know God, we can rest in His justice and power. He wants all sin to be exposed. No matter how it seems in the moment, darkness will not win and the Enemy has nothing on God. Evil will not have the final word, God is not uninvolved, and we will all stand before a just God on judgment day and account for all we've done. That fact comforted me. As Jesus said in the book of John, "I have told you all this so that you may have peace in me. Here on earth you will have many trials and sorrows. But take heart, because I have overcome the world" (16:33).

When we remember that and have an eternal perspective, it can be a little easier to forgive.

The Truth about Forgiveness

The idea and act of forgiveness isn't as cut-and-dried as we'd like it to be. There are many commands throughout the Bible that are fairly black and white, such as "Honor your father and mother" (Ex. 20:12), "Rejoice in the Lord always" (Phil. 4:4 NIV), and "Be quick to listen, slow to speak, and slow to get angry" (James 1:19). But what does God say about forgiveness? "Peter came to him and asked, 'Lord, how often should I forgive someone who sins against me? Seven times?' 'No, not seven times,' Jesus replied, 'but seventy times seven!'" (Matt. 18:21–22).

What I like about Peter's question is how it normalizes the disciples and reveals their humanity. Like me, Peter wanted a hard number, an exact metric of how many times he should forgive. But

that's not what Jesus gave him. What Jesus was getting at is that
there is no magic number for how often we should forgive but that
instead we should extend forgiveness freely.

How can our forgiveness flow freely when we're grinding our
teeth through the pain and holding on to all the details of the hurt
the other person has caused? While it might seem fake to forgive
quickly, I noticed as I held on to the pain and bitterness that I was
still carrying around the past. I don't know about you, but when I
hold on to the past, it's difficult for me to live a life of joy in the Lord.
At the time, I wasn't yet willing to forgive. Something had to shift
in my heart.

Forgiveness Leads to Joy

Because we are human and therefore sinful, it's tempting to rank
the offenses of others and determine that some people flat-out don't
deserve forgiveness. After all, isn't there a huge difference between
someone who cuts us off in traffic and someone who perpetrates
abuse? Likewise, we wouldn't equate someone who forgets a planned
playdate with someone who spreads lies or damaging gossip. I
understand that someone might be having a bad day and cut me off
in traffic. I understand that people can be forgetful. It makes sense
in my mind because I make mistakes too. I accidentally raise my
voice at my kids, or I might be tired and hungry and in turn get mad
at my husband for no reason. But comparing the seriousness of sins
and justifying my sin in light of someone else's won't produce lasting
joy. Instead, it leads to bitterness and pride.

The truth is, we're called to forgive all offenses, small and large.
Because, in the end, it's not about propping ourselves up when we

forgive. It's about surrendering to Christ. As Jesus said, "If you forgive those who sin against you, your heavenly Father will forgive you. But if you refuse to forgive others, your Father will not forgive your sins" (Matt. 6:14–15).

What I've found is that I'm good at forgiveness when it's convenient or involves minor offenses we face every day or relates to the ways I sin against others. Those things I get. That's probably the case for most of us. In those situations, our joy isn't up for grabs. It's when we're tested and stretched, when we have the opportunity to forgive major wrongs against us, that we can either reject the Lord's peace and joy or thrive in it. Forgiveness leads to joy, and "the joy of the LORD is your strength" (Neh. 8:10).

And how do we know that forgiveness brings joy?

First, forgiving someone who wrongs us imitates Christ. Think about Christ on the cross. Even after the abuse and torture He suffered, He still said, "Father, forgive them, for they do not know what they are doing" (Luke 23:34 NIV). The very fact that God was willing to sacrifice His own Son demonstrates His willingness to forgive us for our transgressions (see John 3:16). Also, we are being obedient when we forgive: "Be kind and compassionate to one another, forgiving each other, just as in Christ God forgave you" (Eph. 4:32 NIV). Finally, being obedient and more Christlike will always bring us joy. Not temporary feelings of happiness but lasting joy, an unshakable assurance that we are God's and He loves us.

It's as simple as that. Not always easy, but it is simple.

When we read in Romans 3:23 that "*all* have sinned and fall short of the glory of God" (ESV, emphasis added), we need to remember that God sees every single human as sinful. No one, not a single human being, deserves eternity with the Father. We are all undeserving, and God is so holy that He can't allow *any* sin in His presence. Nothing we could ever do or say or try would get us any closer to an all-holy God.

That's why Jesus will forever be our biggest gift. *Biggest* doesn't even scratch the surface of the magnitude of the cross. It's hard for us to even fathom. God sent His Son and made a way for us to be reconciled to Him. Despite our rebellion, Jesus took our sins on Himself, and God forgave us through His sacrifice and resurrection. And now, if we repent and believe (see Rom. 10:9), we can stand holy and blameless before the Father on judgment day, even though we are weak, broken, and undeserving humans.

That's cause for rejoicing!

But at the same time, when we're in the trenches of unforgiveness, overwhelmed by pain, it's hard to accept these truths for others. It doesn't seem right that we can live our whole lives for Christ, trying to forgive and love others, while another individual, who has lived a degenerate life, can repent on their deathbed, confess that Jesus is Lord, and be rejoicing in heaven with us.

This is one reason the gospel is so hard to live out. But we are called to live in ways that are often counter to the expectations of this world (see Heb. 13:14).

Consider the story of the prodigal son's brother in Luke 15. The younger son chose to leave home and squandered his share of the inheritance. Meanwhile, the older son stayed home with his father, faithfully working in the field. Yet when his younger brother returned and his father celebrated, the older brother said, "Look!

All these years I've been slaving for you and never disobeyed your orders. Yet you never gave me even a young goat so I could celebrate with my friends" (v. 29 NIV).

Can you relate? Have you ever thought *I don't deserve this!* when something bad happens to you? I know I have. I feel a sense of injustice when circumstances don't line up with my personal plans. When I get really caught up in the moment, I can even think that I, a sinner and finite human, know best, even better than the God of the universe.

No honest forgiveness can come from a prideful heart, though. When we forget our place at the foot of the cross, we'll be looking around at everyone else's behavior, trying to impose our story and standards on them.

God is a personal God who relates to each person individually. Each of us will come to understand and believe in Christ on our own timeline, hopefully sooner rather than later. No matter when someone decides to confess and repent, we should be rejoicing. Even if someone abandoned you, betrayed you, hurt you, violated you, or manipulated you, we should rejoice when that person changes and chooses to live out their love for Jesus every day.

Knowing that no one is better than anyone else in the eyes of a holy God humbles me and allows me to see people the way Jesus does. When I started to understand my own sin, I could look at these men who hurt me and see them as sinners who needed Jesus like I did. While what they did was horrific, I can't let their sin affect my joyful life and get me offtrack. Forgiving someone is a gift not only to that person but to yourself as well.

A Life of Forgiveness

Years later, I was still trying to understand the process of forgiveness. The truth is that, while learning forgiveness was a long and difficult journey for me with my dad, my coach, and the man who raped me, it was "easier" to forgive them in the long run. Let me explain. For starters, I saw a major heart change in my dad; he thoroughly rededicated his life to the Lord and is now a completely different person. It makes sense to forgive someone who changes. For some reason, it validates the weight of forgiveness, and you feel lighter when you know that the person hurt you because he or she wasn't following Jesus.

Secondly, my volleyball coach passed away. While that's terribly sad, I no longer live in the fear of running into him. I could work through the pain, forgive, and release it to the Lord.

And lastly, I was able to forgive the man who raped me because I knew that he would have to give an account before God for what he did to me. That brought me so much closer to the Lord because I knew He would always be both loving and just. Understanding God's true character brings not only joy but also comfort. Then, with time and a lot of counseling, I saw God bring me so much peace through each of those circumstances. I know it's cheesy, but time really does heal.

But recently, all these years later, I was sitting at my desk job struggling to forgive in another relationship. *I thought I already learned how to forgive?* What I soon realized was that forgiveness needed to be a part of my *daily* life, especially when I didn't see the kinds of outcomes I had before.

In my opinion, forgiveness is ten times harder when there's no change, no apology, or no resolution, all while both parties are claiming to follow Jesus. That is when you have to choose forgiveness daily. If I wanted to live a life of joy, it wasn't going to be a one-and-done kind of thing for me but a moment-by-moment practice. Just as we need daily grace from others and the Lord, there will always be people who hurt us and need our forgiveness as well. My forgiveness journey wasn't over, and I started making excuses for not forgiving others in my life, such as:

> *I don't want my quick forgiveness to be taken for approval of the divisive actions of others.*
> *My act of love through forgiveness could enable the hurt to continue.*
> *Forgiving will merely shove my deep pain under the surface.*
> *Forgiveness might negate the need for consequences of bad behavior.*

Maybe you've thought these same things. Since I thought my forgiveness cup was overflowing after all these years, I started to hold on to the negativity that this lack of forgiveness brought back into my life. I felt the same feelings of insecurity, pain, heartbreak, injustice, and bitterness beginning to fester inside me, just as they had all those years before.

Suddenly, one of the company's counselors rushing by my desk noticed I was wrestling with something. (Side note: people will always notice if you're a bitter, judgmental person or someone living free and joyfully.) He asked if I was okay, and I briefly shared how difficult it was to forgive those who claim to love Jesus yet continue to cause so many people pain.

He raised his eyebrows and said, "Not forgiving them, regardless of what they have done or the pain they have caused, is going to be poison to your soul. You want them to apologize, but every day you wait and don't forgive, you are continuing to drink the poison."

At the time, I honestly thought he was being a little dramatic. *I was fine, everything was fine.* I also wanted to defend myself, saying, "But they said this" or "They did this," as if that would change his response.

It's a constant choice to let God's justice prevail, whether I see it in this lifetime or not.

I let my guard down, and when I wasn't trusting God to defend and protect me, I felt the need to take matters into my own hands and be my own defender, protector, and judge by withholding my forgiveness. Talk about a joy stealer! It's a constant choice to let God's justice prevail, whether I see it in this lifetime or not.

Cultivating a forgiving heart must become a daily practice. Although it is often more popular to do the opposite, to seek vengeance instead of forgiveness, all that does is stir up bitterness and dissatisfaction. The true justice we're craving will come, but not from us. It's God's job.

Living Unoffended

In seeking to emulate Christ, we should live unoffended. When we walk around with offended hearts, we haven't grasped that all sinful acts done *to us* or *by us* are ultimately against God (see Ps. 51:4–5). If we remain offended and refuse to forgive, we're letting the world influence our behavior by harboring bitterness. When people hurt us, no matter how personal it *feels*, their salvation and heart motivations are between them and God.

It's impossible to be both easily offended *and* ready to forgive. We're essentially saying we don't trust God to be both loving and just. Instead, we're setting ourselves up to be our own saviors and judges, determining who deserves our forgiveness.

That, my friends, is a nasty, sad, dark place to live. I was there for far too long. It's exhausting too, because unforgiveness clouds your whole perspective and life. If we can humble ourselves and see that Jesus forgave us at our worst, then we can forgive that person who wronged us, regardless of what he or she did.

After years of wanting to take back my freedom and joy despite the heaviness I was facing, asking myself the following questions— and answering them honestly—allowed me to release the pain and move forward:

- *Am I being obedient to Christ and forgiving those who hurt me?*

- *Am I playing the victim and allowing the pain caused by others to dictate my life?*
- *Am I modeling my behavior after Christ in the process?*
- *Am I living unoffended?*
- *Am I surrendering to God, the ultimate judge?*

When I considered my response to each of those questions, my joy was slowly restored. I couldn't change anyone or make someone apologize. Ultimately, God is on His throne and I had to trust that all wrongs *will* be made right someday. Choosing to fight for this eternal perspective brings me so much joy and enables me to forgive.

Choosing to fight for this eternal perspective brings me so much joy and enables me to forgive.

And let me say this to you, friends: Too many times as Christians we think we have to be chummy with everyone because we love Jesus. Yes, we're called to live at peace with everyone (see Rom. 12:18), but sometimes joy will be found when you finally say, "I forgive you, but you can no longer be involved in my life." You are not unholy or weak if you've been advised by counselors or the Holy Spirit to walk away from dysfunction, narcissism, toxic relationships, or abuse. Sacrificing your purpose, joy, and peace to play along with someone else's problems will keep you in a perpetual state of people-pleasing instead of living free. You answer to the Lord, and although He's calling you to forgive, sometimes taking back your joy calls for setting healthy boundaries between yourself and those offenders.

In her book *Forgiving What You Can't Forget*, Lysa TerKeurst wrote, "You don't want to trade in your peace, your maturity, your spiritual progress, your integrity, and all the other beauty you add to the world just to add a little suffering to your offender's life or to try and teach them a lesson."[1] I love that.

That's so beautiful because it takes us out of the mess and has us looking at the bigger picture of what God is doing. While it may be difficult to admit, sometimes we get so wrapped up in our pain that we want to sit in it rather than let go of it, forgive, and move on. As Christians, we can find it more meaningful to suffer and to be battling hard times. We can hold on to our problems longer than we should in order to have something to talk about with our friends, spouses, or communities. This attitude perpetuates victimhood as opposed to joyful, victorious living.

God wants us to live lives of freedom and love and purpose and joy. We may need to surrender offenses, pride, insecurities, pain, or a record of wrongs if we don't want to live one more day in bitterness. While that can feel like a tall order, we have the strength to accomplish this through Christ.

This may not be a quick process. Sometimes we need counseling or a daily reminder to choose forgiveness. And reconciliation is not guaranteed. Just because *you* follow Jesus doesn't mean you should let people continue to hurt and abuse you, regardless of whether *they* claim to be "Christian" or not. We can learn forgiveness without enabling others to continue in their sin. There is much joy in seeing a restored and changed heart. But perhaps the greatest joy and peace is found when we step back and allow God to judge, freeing us to process our pain with the Holy Spirit.

Obviously, I haven't seen every wrong done to me exposed and corrected. But there are snippets of hope. My father has been reconciled to our family, and our relationship restored. Not only did he walk me down the aisle (even though I'd told him that would never happen), but God also redeemed my parents' marriage. Now I have the great joy of witnessing the fruits produced from forgiveness, a changed heart, and the hand of God.

Although it took way longer than I would have liked (I'm not the best at patience), I was also able to forgive and finally release the anger and bitterness I felt in other relationships. As I recognized my own sin and need for forgiveness, it made the choice to step aside and let God work on my behalf a little easier. God will judge accordingly, and we can do our part by choosing to make forgiveness a daily practice so that we can live unoffended and free.

Remember that we serve a faithful and just God who will give us glimpses of the joy that can come from forgiveness and the Holy Spirit's work. Not all the time. But when we trust Him, we will see moments of joy as we forgive.

I pray that today we can forgive the people who have wronged us regardless of the offense. Let's forgive, hold tight to the promise of God's redemptive work, and choose freedom so the joy we're all searching for will flow freely.

reflections

Take Action

Do you have unforgiveness in your heart? Forgiving someone who wronged us is often a daily choice. Make that choice today so you can be free of bitterness. Recognize your own sinfulness, and remember that we are all undeserving of the love of a holy God. Choose forgiveness as an act of obedience.

Key Verse

"Do not take revenge, my dear friends, but leave room for God's wrath, for it is written: 'It is mine to avenge; I will repay,' says the Lord." (Rom. 12:19 NIV)

Closing Prayer

Lord, I confess my struggle to forgive. Because of the pain I've faced, I am having the hardest time letting go. Forgive me. I know You are sovereign and You took on all my sin. Although I am undeserving, I pray that Your grace and forgiveness will wash over me. Help me extend grace to others and forgive quickly. Please guide, direct, and lead me. You are a merciful God. I choose to trust that You will make all things right and You will always be just. Help me forgive those who have wronged me. Thank You for loving me despite my sin and for Your unending love and forgiveness. Keep me seeking after You, Lord, and help me to do the right thing even when it's difficult.

serve others

Say Goodbye to Perfection

When I'm crawling through the darkest trenches of life, all I want to do is eat some cookies, hide in my room, wear sweatpants, cry, and binge-watch a new favorite show to distract me from my depressing reality. Basically, the last thing I want to do during pain or difficulty is to serve someone else. How's that for honest?

But when I look back on my life, it's evident that God has used me to serve others during my own hardships. I see how He orchestrated circumstances that forced me to focus on others instead of myself. He provided serving opportunities in the midst of my own battles so I could start to see a bigger picture of what God was doing around me.

I already shared that the months after I was raped were some of the hardest I've faced. I was dealing with the sexual assault, processing the betrayal and lies from my dad, struggling to forgive others, and trying to function normally. I was in the thick of my senior year of college, and each time I thought I'd made it through the fire, another trial came.

How in the world was I supposed to deal with familial pain, keep up with the ongoing police investigation, go to counseling, fill my role as captain of my volleyball team, and try to finish my senior year of college? I felt as if there were nowhere to run, no one to run to, and nothing to keep me afloat, and worst of all, I felt that God had abandoned me as well.

I was spiraling downward very quickly.

Less than two months after the assault, the head of women's ministries and missions at our college group, Julia, called me. She wanted to meet in her office to talk. I immediately started sweating, thinking she was going to question my involvement at church. I'm sure she had noticed I was the last to show up to our college group meetings and the first to leave. I didn't want to talk to anyone during that time. Silently suffering can do that to you—it can isolate you when you need people the most.

I'm sure she had also observed changes in me. My personality was no longer bubbly and talkative. I wasn't showing up early to help with setup, greeting everyone with a big smile, or talking to dozens of people throughout the evening.

After putting it off for a short time, I finally scheduled a meeting with Julia. Once I arrived at her office, I was nervous all over again. I felt like I needed to apologize for not being my normal self. Part of me just wanted to cry and let it all out right there in her cozy guest chair, while the other part wanted to pretend like nothing had ever happened.

We made small talk for a couple of minutes, and then Julia said, "Nicole, I want you to lead the missions trip to Nepal next summer."

I was completely stunned. I thought, *You've got to be kidding me. Boy, is she in for a surprise when she hears about my insane life.*

I immediately burst into tears and said, "Absolutely not." Instead of feeling excited for the opportunity, feelings of failure and a running list of painful memories flooded my mind.

The college coach who never gave me a chance.

The Christian campus director who said I'd never be a good leader.

The boy who used me.

The dad who failed me.

The counselor who hit on me.

The academic probation.

The rape.

The verbal abuse.

Who was I to lead a team? I knew that when she heard about my recent experiences, Julia would certainly second-guess her decision and rescind her invitation.

Still, I hesitated to share what I was walking through. I thought that if I told Julia everything, I'd have to add her to the list of people who hurt me, reminding me of all the pain I had to endure. I wasn't ready for another disappointment, assuming she'd regret her decision and backpedal, saying, "You're right. You are too messed up. I'll choose someone better." That would hurt too much.

After I told her no, Julia didn't even ask why. She just repeated herself. "Nicole, I want you to lead the missions trip!" As if declaring it once again would change my mind.

I knew I had to tell her why this couldn't happen so we could move on and I could get out of that office. Through tears, I shared why I felt I wasn't equipped to lead and suggested that she pick a more spiritual girl, one who really had her life together. I told her the details of my shattered circumstances, the pain I was walking through, the doubt I was feeling, and the depression that was slowly taking over my soul.

Her response forever changed me.

"I'm so sorry you're walking through this, Nicole, but God wants you to lead this team. You are broken and have nothing to offer, so I know God will step in and work in huge ways. Let Him be your strength and wisdom. Let Him heal you and lead you so you can be the best leader."

In that moment, she saw me as Jesus did. Broken and weak, but also a vessel that could be used if I said yes and submitted.

I get emotional every time I think of that day, because I was so humbled, honored, and terrified at the same time. This was the moment when God began redeeming and mending my unraveled life.

> ## She saw me as Jesus did. Broken and weak, but also a vessel that could be used if I said yes and submitted.

Julia told me to pray about it, but I knew before I got back in my car that this was what God wanted. He wanted to redeem a past situation, protect me as I embraced a new role, and renew my perspective of Him, showing me where my strength originates. When it felt as if I had nowhere to go and no one to turn to, God revealed that He was all I needed.

Friends, He uses *all* things for our good (see Rom. 8:28 NIV). Often, when we're in the middle of our own struggles, we can't see it. But don't we know that He can use us in our weakness so that His power may be displayed? Second Corinthians 12:9–10 says:

> He said to me, "My grace is sufficient for you, for my power is made perfect in weakness." Therefore I will boast all the more gladly about my weaknesses, so that Christ's power may rest on me. That is why, for Christ's sake, I delight in weaknesses, in insults, in hardships, in persecutions, in difficulties. For when I am weak, then I am strong. (NIV)

I now know that Julia was going through a lot at the time as well. We all have our own baggage and burdens, but she chose to see the best in me, viewing me as God does. She displayed such grace and tenderness despite her own trials, when I'm sure she could have used a dose of grace and tenderness herself.

Her example of leadership showed me that meeting people where they are, in their brokenness, was how I wanted to lead and serve going forward. Having someone believe in me despite my weaknesses and all I'd been through changed my perspective on life, second chances, and God's redeeming and loving power in our lives. Experiences like that make me want to be more selfless.

Serving in Spite of Pain

What if we were all more like that? What if whenever we were down in the dumps, we chose to love on others and serve the people right in front of us? Let's start meeting people where they are, in their chaos and loneliness, their financial strain, or their broken-ness. Instead of trying to prove how amazing we are and how called we are to lead, we should humble ourselves and admit our own struggles.

We need to remember how desperately we *each* need Jesus.

The best leaders find common ground and make you feel seen and valued while also calling you to holiness. I determined right then that I wouldn't lead out of a sense of pride, perfection, or supe-rior knowledge. Leaders serve.

I believe God uses our pain for a higher purpose: to bring other people closer to Him. Sometimes we don't even know it. Maybe the darkness we're walking through will provide light for someone else so they don't feel so isolated in their own trials. Shared experiences have power, and when we understand we're not alone, we can get through the day.

Jesus is the greatest example of serving others while walking through His own battles. Matthew 20:28 says, "Even the Son of Man came not to be served but to serve others and to give his life as a ransom for many." Throughout His life, Jesus served through miracles and lessons, healing and teaching many. He served and listened to those who were discounted by society, washing their feet and pointing them to truth. Every day of Jesus' life was filled with service; even as He hung on the cross, He was making sure His mother would be looked after and the man on His right would be with Him in eternity (see John 19:26–27; Luke 23:32–43).

While in the most excruciating pain—physically, spiritually, emotionally, and mentally—feeling separated from His Father, bearing the weight of the entire world, Christ *still chose* to die for you and me. We were on His mind when we deserved it the least, yet His act of love and service saved anyone who believes and puts their trust in Him. Anyone.

I am so glad Jesus didn't take a rain check that day. I'm so glad He didn't hide away while eating manna and honey, pushing everyone away and just having a "me" day. I'm so glad Jesus trusted His Father enough to carry out His plan, despite fully knowing everything He would have to go through. I'm so thankful that the awful circumstances and His painful reality didn't get in the way of fulfilling His sovereign purpose.

If we are supposed to exemplify Christ, then we should be serving even in our suffering. This doesn't mean pushing aside our problems or forgoing healing. Nor does it mean faking our way through or serving others instead of dealing with our own pain. Rather, as we allow the Spirit to guide us and submit to our own healing process, we ask Him to make our lives an offering to Him.

Maybe you're thinking, *But that's too much to ask, Nicole!* I get it. Our selfish natures want nothing to do with serving others. The world screams *self-care, self-love, you do you, save yourself, you deserve it,* and *make everything about yourself.* Who doesn't feel better temporarily when we focus on ourselves? I know I do! But if we make things about ourselves all the time, we'll be stuck in a victim mentality when trials come, asking questions such as "Why did this happen to me?" or "Why doesn't God love me?"

A self-focus will make it difficult to find answers to "why" questions, since our sufferings are never personal. Yet we take things so personally because we were born thinking only about ourselves. We often rationalize self-focused activities as contributing to our healing when we're really indulging ourselves.

When hard things come, we need to remember that Christ sees our service to others as an offering to Him. Following Jesus means opposing the things of the world. When we truly know Him, we understand that He's calling us to something greater, something outside ourselves but much more beneficial for us in the long run.

Rescued by Service

After being assigned a leadership role for this international missions trip, I felt I needed to step up my "spiritual game." Since I would be leading other students, I felt I needed to be a stronger Christian. Instead, I felt so inadequate and unprepared. I had to remember that God chose me. Despite my brokenness, He chose me, picked me up, set my feet on solid ground, and was now using me to expand His kingdom. I resonated with this passage from the book of Psalms:

> I waited patiently for the LORD to help me,
>   and he turned to me and heard my cry.
> He lifted me out of the pit of despair,
>   out of the mud and the mire.
> He set my feet on solid ground
>   and steadied me as I walked along.

> He has given me a new song to sing,
>> a hymn of praise to our God.
> Many will see what he has done and be amazed.
>> They will put their trust in the LORD. (40:1–3)

God knew I needed something to draw me even closer to Him right when I was considering walking away. He knew I needed a way to heal, and it became so evident to me that God was at work when I needed Him the most. While I felt abandoned, He was already one step ahead of me, showing me the way.

If we take a step back and look around, we see opportunities to serve everywhere. We just have to ask God where He wants to use us. If we're not pouring our lives out for Him, then what or who are we living for?

I've heard it said that God can't heal you if you don't think you need to be healed. We are all in need of a Savior, and when we understand who our King is and His purpose for us, humility will be the crux of our relationship with Him and others. When we understand that our lives are not our own, serving others in our suffering should come naturally, right?

Wrong. At least for me.

Living for Jesus can feel like a backward experience. Do the opposite of what the world is telling you, and you're on the right path. For example, the world says that you can save yourself, that you should pull yourself up by your bootstraps, do the right thing and "karma" will reward you, or just buy a bunch of things to make yourself happy. But what we're missing is always Jesus. He is the only one who can fulfill the gaping hole in our lives and save our souls.

Remember, Christianity is not a works-based religion. We can never *do* enough to make it to heaven. It is only by grace that we have been saved (see Eph. 2:8), and Jesus paves the way (see John 14:6). Until we accept the lost state of our souls, we can't come to terms with new life. This redeemed life starts when we choose to do the opposite of what the world expects. So when trials come our way, we respond by serving others instead of focusing on ourselves.

Sometimes this makes no logical sense and is extremely difficult to do because our sinful nature is weak and we want what we want. Even Paul acknowledged this difficulty: "I know that good itself does not dwell in me, that is, in my sinful nature. For I have the desire to do what is good, but I cannot carry it out" (Rom. 7:18 NIV).

> **Not only in seasons of pain but throughout our entire lives, we can choose to live for the good of others and to display God's glory.**

While serving is important and sometimes the bridge that helps us cross over from pain to purpose, some bridges aren't meant to be crossed right away. I would prefer to be healed right away. (Wouldn't everyone?) But it's critical to prayerfully evaluate where you are on your healing journey so you don't step out in service too soon. True joy is found when we submit to God's will and walk with Him daily, even when healing is painful and takes time. Healing looks different for everyone, so walk slowly with purpose, one foot in front of the other.

Serving others through our pain starts with understanding that God wants to use us. The light we have because of Christ can be an example of Him to everyone we meet, even during difficult times. When we realize our lives are offerings to the Lord, we want to pour them out for Christ and accomplish the will of the Father. Not because we *have* to, but because we *get* to partner with Him and find fulfillment and lasting joy.

Not only in seasons of pain but throughout our entire lives, we can choose to live for the good of others and to display God's glory. Instead of living for ourselves as the world demands, we can decide to live lives of complete service that are *for* and *about* the King. But this daily act of surrender can be difficult. I intentionally have to work to live a more selfless life, because it doesn't come naturally, especially when I'm going through my own challenges.

In our me-centered world, we must ask God to show us how we can bless others and be used by Him. Because even in our darkest moments, we can be lights. We don't have to have it all together. We don't have to look and feel and act perfect to be used by Him. God meets us where we are in our burdens and struggles and is so faithful to use us in both big and small ways. He doesn't have to, but He chooses to present opportunities to use us to love and serve others.

Let's not forget that serving can be a thankless task. There have been many days when no one thanked me. I wiped bottoms, cooked meals, drove everyone around, brought snacks for sports practice, and nursed in the middle of the night. Moms don't get thanked, though. But don't lose heart, because serving others will bring joy and, while unseen, is noticed by God: "Give your gifts in private, and your Father, who sees everything, will reward you" (Matt. 6:4).

Perfection Not Required

Recently I was reading about Abram in the book of Genesis. Before God gave him a new name, he was a mess. He was selfish and a sinner, just like you and me, and constantly took matters into his own hands instead of trusting God. Yet God chose him to be the father of as many descendants as there are stars in the heavens (see 26:4). Ultimately, "God chooses people according to his own purposes; he calls people, but not according to their good or bad works" (Rom. 9:11–12).

The story of Abram demonstrates that nothing can thwart God's plan. If He calls us and we're walking in His will, we can be part of it. In the Lord's Prayer, we are instructed to ask for God's will to be done: "Your kingdom come, your will be done, on earth as it is in heaven" (Matt. 6:10 NIV). That is what we all should want: to be used by God to accomplish His will.

And the best news is that God uses people despite their flaws. David was known as a man after God's own heart (see 1 Sam. 13:14), and Jesus came from his lineage. The Lord used David to defeat Goliath, which led to the defeat of the Philistine army (see 1 Sam. 17) and David's ascension to the throne of Israel. Yet David was deeply flawed and had Uriah killed to cover his sin after sleeping with Uriah's wife, Bathsheba (see 2 Sam. 11).

Peter was a close follower of Jesus, a defender of the faith who took the gospel to many places. Yet he also cut off a servant's ear in defense of Christ (see John 18:10), doubted that Jesus would rescue him (see Matt. 14:31), and denied Jesus three times (see Luke 22:54–62).

Noah was "a righteous man [who] walked faithfully with God" (Gen. 6:9 NIV) and was chosen to rescue a remnant from God's judgment, yet he was a drunkard and brought shame on his family (see 9:21–23).

> **While we are all undeserving of God's love and redemption, He still gives us the opportunity to participate in the work of His kingdom.**

I could go on with many more biblical examples of human weakness, such as Sarah's lack of trust, Saul's hatred toward and persecution of Christians, Adam and Eve's disobedience, and the promiscuity of the woman at the well. These stories illustrate that everyone makes mistakes, yet each of our lives matters to God. While we are all undeserving of God's love and redemption, He still gives us the opportunity to participate in the work of His kingdom, ultimately giving us purpose and fulfillment through glorifying Him.

No matter our past, we can see a thread of Jesus working in our lives. Often God uses us when we least expect it so that His strength and glory might be displayed. He continues to pursue us even though we might be questioning or enduring hard circumstances.

It's in that sweet spot of contentment through service that true joy can be found. Living a victorious life in Christ starts with serving others. I had no idea as a twenty-two-year-old that God would use leadership and service to usher in a season of healing.

Before we left on our trip, I began praying for each member of my team and supporting each of them in any way I could. I made it my mission to invest in them so they felt fully equipped and ready to love and serve all those we met. And you know what I found? When I focused on them, it seemed as if my own personal pain started to subside. My burdens became lighter as our team shared in each other's sufferings (see Rom. 12:15). Serving my team members before we had even left our own country helped me realize I wasn't the only person going through something difficult. Everyone is fighting a battle and can use extra prayer and support (we all just need to admit it).

When we arrived in Nepal, God used my brokenness and weakness to meet my new friends in their own brokenness. What I found in the place of shared pain was that my own pain receded. While I still felt like my life was in shambles at times, I also became more aware of my privilege as an American, a land of opportunity, wealth, and freedom. My new Nepalese friends faced a reality that was quite the opposite. That realization increased my gratitude for all that God has given me and all that He has walked me through. Serving reminded me that "God's got this" and that He would continue to walk with me all my days.

Now whenever I walk through trials, I ask God to provide ways to serve so that I remain close to Jesus. In a similar way, I pray God gives you opportunities to serve as He starts to heal the brokenness you thought would never be fixed. If you're walking through a season of suffering, I'm so sorry. You may feel like you have nothing to offer, but God can step in and work in huge ways through you. Let Him be your strength and wisdom. God isn't after perfection, so come as you are and watch how He works. Let Him heal you and lead you so you can be His faithful servant.

reflections

Take Action

Look around and identify one or two ways you could serve those around you. Is it in your family, your community, your church, or your neighborhood? It's so easy to focus on ourselves when trials come our way. But ask the Lord to provide a chance this week for you to focus on others and serve joyfully.

Key Verse

"God chooses people according to his own purposes; he calls people, but not according to their good or bad works." (Rom. 9:11–12)

Closing Prayer

Lord, thank You for being the best example of a suffering servant. Despite my pain, please open my eyes to the needs of those around me. Provide opportunities in the coming days for me to serve so that my focus shifts from myself to others. I pray that You would use my weaknesses to display Your glory and that even when I'm at my worst, Your power would be made known. Thank You for laying Your Son's life down for me. I ask for that same selfless heart going forward.

adjust your perspective

Freshly Baked Cookies

Do you ever have those moments when you're so thankful for all the blessings God has given you that you just sit and cry with gratitude? And then just as fast, something horrible can happen and all you want is to be united with Christ in heaven so the sadness and tears will be no more?

A few years ago, I met two of my best friends for a girls' weekend away. I left my three boys at home with my husband and embarked on a solo adventure. Flying without kids seemed magical. There I was, strolling around the airport on a layover with only one bag, taking bathroom breaks alone, and even holding a still-warm coffee with one hand free. It was a thrill for this busy boy-mom.

I had a great time with my friends. And the best part was, I had just found out before hopping on the plane that I was pregnant with our fourth baby! I hadn't told anyone yet. This would be our last baby, so I was planning a grand announcement for our family and friends when I returned home.

We sang in the car (not to Disney songs), ate some fantastic food (not prepared by me), and caught up on life (without interruption). That weekend was a refreshing interlude in my chaotic month. I even bought a cute summer dress that would be perfect for my growing baby bump. I was soaking up the sunshine and savoring every moment with my friends. I was so grateful to my husband, Andrew, for making this getaway happen despite his crazy medical school schedule.

One evening as my friends and I walked back from a little outdoor restaurant, I felt a small gush. *Am I bleeding? What is happening? I've never bled during pregnancy before.* I needed to get back to the rental house.

We arrived at the house and, sure enough, I was bleeding. I was shocked, crying nonstop, but still had some hope that this could be normal. We stayed put until my flight the next day, sitting on the couch eating chocolate chip cookies as I tried to believe everything would be okay.

So much was going on in that season of my life. Even on the best days, life could bring a dose of sadness. The positive and negative in our lives are so intertwined, and sometimes all I do is focus on the negative. As that weekend ended, I was thankful for the fun trip but also worried every second about what might happen when I saw a doctor. I swung from extremely carefree and joyful to down in the dumps within a span of minutes.

When I got home, I scheduled an appointment with my doctor and took a pregnancy test. The test was still clearly positive, so I started to have more hope. *Maybe this is just implantation bleeding?*

Maybe this is normal for some women, or maybe this is some kind of fourth-pregnancy thing?

When I finally got to my appointment, the ultrasound showed there was still something forming in my belly. However, the midwife told me I was probably going through a miscarriage based on my dates. I started bawling. She reassured me that it wasn't my fault and asked me to come back in two weeks to make sure this forming baby had "passed."

I left so confused because I saw with my own eyes that my uterus was, in fact, not empty. I couldn't fully grieve because I was still holding on to the slight chance that everything was fine. Maybe I would go back for my next appointment to find a heartbeat. God is a God of miracles, right? I was determined to prove that midwife wrong. God's glory would be revealed. We're supposed to have hope and faith and expect God to do great things, and I knew He was going to come through. What a great story this would be!

The next morning was Match Day for Andrew. In the fourth year of medical school, this is when you find out where you're going for residency (the next phase of training). You don't get to pick where you end up. The emcee counted down, "Five, four, three, two, one! Open your envelopes!" We ripped his open and found out we were moving to North Carolina, across the country and away from my parents, our best friends, and our church community. We had hoped to continue his training in Colorado and were shocked to see another location.

I thought, *What the heck is God doing? I can't move away from all my family and friends and have a miscarriage at the same time ... It would all be too much.*

Regardless, we started packing up our house in preparation for the move. I still felt pregnant and was hopeful. Hesitant but hopeful. This baby was going to be okay.

In those two weeks before my next appointment, I started planning again. I was checking out my favorite baby shops and looking at houses in North Carolina with enough rooms for all our children. I knew God was a miracle worker and could save this baby.

But that was not His plan.

On the day of my appointment, I woke up to two little boys crawling into bed with me. There was a beautiful sunrise, and I told God, "I want what You want. I want my life to align with Your plan. And I want whatever brings You the most glory."

As I walked into the doctor's office, I truly thought it was going to be a day of rejoicing. In my mind, hearing a healthy heartbeat on the monitor would definitely bring God the most glory.

I got undressed and lay on the table, holding Andrew's hand. The first ultrasound tech found … nothing. There was nothing on the screen. No blood, no amniotic sac, no extra fluid, no infection, no baby. Absolutely nothing.

The second technician came in and saw the same thing. Nothing. After three people checked me, I knew it was over. My uterus was empty.

They asked me to come back a couple of weeks later for blood work to make sure my levels had returned to normal. If they hadn't, I'd have to have a surgical procedure to ensure my uterus was empty. That was it. I had officially had a miscarriage.

I was devastated, and honestly, I still get sad when I think about it. Why couldn't I have just had a negative pregnancy test from the beginning? It seemed like a cruel prank, like someone gave me the best present but then took it away a few weeks later after I was already attached to it. Why would God do something like that?

My heart hardened that day. With all I had already walked through, you would think that nothing could have shaken me, but I was instantly afraid that this specific crack in my faith would completely ruin me. After all the planning and excitement, I couldn't accept what was happening. Why did God allow this miscarriage? Not only was I left questioning God again, but a part of me was gone. I was overwhelmed with heartache and left with a cold emptiness.

The same week as my miscarriage, Andrew and I hopped on a plane to search for a home in North Carolina. Instead of being excited for a trip alone with him, I was still grieving our loss. I felt numb. No matter what was going on around me, it didn't matter as much as my broken heart and shattered dreams. How was I supposed to be elated about finding a new house when I was still in sorrow over this loss?

God with Us

I told myself to keep going, just keep moving. What else could I do? Life doesn't stop for those dealing with heartbreak. I still had a to-do list the length of a football field, especially with the move coming up. It wasn't exactly easy to pack up a house all by myself with our three little boys under the age of four hanging on me while my husband was at work.

When I was younger, my dad changed jobs frequently and would move us to a new state every three years or so. Moving that frequently helped me love change. I discovered there were two roads

I could walk: acceptance or regret. As a kid, I could either accept the change and learn to thrive in my new environment or remain stuck, wishing I were still living in the past. While it may sound like I was wise beyond my years, it was really my desire to decorate a new bedroom every few years that led me to embrace acceptance every time.

But now, all these years later, this move with my own family seemed like too much change all at once. Too much for me to handle.

Our lives became filled with cardboard boxes and Bubble Wrap. We said our goodbyes, especially goodbye to the little house that had been our safe haven for the last three years. With every box I packed, treasured memories filled my mind. I would throw some toys and kids' clothes into a box, and a flood of birthdays and holidays would rush in as I sealed the flap with packing tape. The trip back from the hospital after our third son was born ... the best couch-and-blanket forts ... playing hide-and-seek in the dark with dinosaur headlamps ... dance parties and family naps. It was the perfect house for that season of our lives, and I was filled with gratitude tinged with sorrow.

With each new morning that came, I still didn't know what to feel or how to act. I was so excited about a new house but devastated to leave our community. I was ready for change but filled with grief for our lost baby. So many emotions. How was I supposed to get through this?

I needed to switch my focus to gain a fresh perspective. Not dismissing the reality of what was happening or faking a smile and acting like I was fine, but embracing it *all*. Embracing each emotion when it came and not apologizing for it. Embracing each moment for what it was, good or bad. Remaining hopeful for the future while dealing with pain at the same time. Putting one foot in front of the other and walking slowly through each day. I found comfort in the following verse:

> The LORD your God in your midst,
> The Mighty One, will save;
> He will rejoice over you with gladness,
> He will quiet you with His love,
> He will rejoice over you with singing. (Zeph. 3:17 NKJV)

I found comfort in knowing God was with me. You can take comfort in this truth as well. No one understands the weight of the world—including the sorrow, loss, and devastation we face—more than Jesus. We can lean on Him. The one thing we know is that He is always with us, orchestrating a bigger plan than we could imagine.

God Is Faithful

In this season, when I felt as if life was an unending series of ups and downs, I was encouraged by reading about the life of Joseph in Genesis 37–50. His life is one of the best biblical examples of someone who had extremely high highs alternating with the lowest lows.

First we learn that Joseph grew up in a large family in Canaan. He was Jacob's second-youngest son and his father's favorite. His brothers grew jealous of him and considered killing him, but instead, they threw him into a cistern, after which they sold him into slavery. Meanwhile, God was working on Joseph's behalf, as He always is for us.

Joseph was eventually sold to Potiphar, an official in the government of Pharaoh, the king of Egypt. Joseph succeeded in everything he did as he served in the home of his Egyptian master. He was a young man who had experienced great loss and betrayal, but God chose to bring about restoration through his service to Potiphar. I'm sure Joseph missed his father and homeland greatly, but God was with him through all of it.

Eventually Joseph was promoted to be Potiphar's personal attendant and put in charge of the whole household. Because God was blessing Joseph, Potiphar began to prosper as well. Everything went well until Potiphar's wife began pressuring Joseph to sleep with her. Although Joseph remained strong and resisted her, Potiphar's wife falsely accused Joseph of attempted rape. Can you imagine? I'm sure Joseph thought, *I can't catch a break!* Joseph was doing the right thing, but Potiphar believed his wife and had Joseph thrown into prison.

I guarantee Joseph did not want to be in prison, yet even then the Lord showed up when all seemed lost. Genesis 39:21 says, "The LORD was with Joseph in the prison and showed him his faithful love. And the LORD made Joseph a favorite with the prison warden." With God's help, Joseph interpreted dreams for two other prisoners, but it was two more years before he was called on to interpret Pharaoh's dreams. What a long wait! Joseph probably wondered where God was and whether He had forsaken him. But because Joseph interpreted Pharaoh's dreams when all the wise men of Egypt had failed, Pharaoh promoted him to a powerful position again as his second-in-command. God continued to provide for Joseph.

When famine came to Egypt and the surrounding countries, Egypt was prepared because Joseph had been stockpiling grain. Meanwhile, Joseph's brothers were in need of food and traveled to Egypt to buy it. When they came before Joseph, he recognized them immediately and decided to test them. He accused them of being spies and put them in prison for three days, where the brothers' guilt festered. God intervened and allowed a wrong to be corrected. I don't know about you, but I am so thankful when I'm able to witness God correcting a wrong in my life. Maybe that's my justice-driven personality, but I imagine Joseph finally felt like someone was on his side. Joseph was even able to see his brother Benjamin again and wept with joy.

What is most astounding to me about this story is that Joseph said to his brothers, "It was God who sent me here ahead of you to preserve your lives" (45:5). Then he reaffirmed his stance in this oft-quoted verse: "You intended to harm me, but God intended it all for good. He brought me to this position so I could save the lives of many people" (50:20).

Instead of placing blame on his brothers, Joseph clearly understood that God was the one who had led him during all those years. I can't say I'd do the same thing in the moment, but every story throughout Joseph's life points to Jesus. Joseph's brothers deserved to be punished for the way they had treated him. Instead, Joseph showed them grace and love, just as Jesus does for each of us. While we should be punished for our sin, God made a way.

Although Joseph experienced extreme trials, such as betrayal, heartache, and imprisonment, he also experienced power, prosperity, relational peace, and restoration. He knew that God was with him through it all and that there was a greater purpose at work. While I imagine Joseph was extremely frustrated and mad at times, he accepted each trial and remained confident in God's sovereignty and provision.

This is so encouraging to me. We can choose how to view our lives and what we assume about ourselves and about God. Sometimes I overspiritualize my pain and project all my emotions onto God. Instead of remaining faithful and consistent, I have been quick to question Him. Because I'm a Christian, I assumed God would treat me differently and not allow as much suffering. But as we know, that's simply not true. Our trials do not negate God's love for us. Rather, it's the pain that typically draws us to Him.

C. S. Lewis wrote, "The great thing, if one can, is to stop regarding all the unpleasant things as interruptions of one's 'own' or 'real' life. The truth is of course that what one calls interruptions are precisely one's real life—the life God is sending one day by day."[1] How much longer was I going to be shocked that hard things came my way?

The secret I started to discover was that trials have fostered my growth in God. Suffering has built my character. Do I wish for tribulations? No. Do I like trials? Absolutely not! But I am so grateful that God loves me enough to walk with me through them and restore my joy in spite of them.

Each of us is dealt a hand of cards in life, and instead of throwing them down, giving up, trading them in, or wishing we had a different hand, we can switch our focus to God's faithfulness. We can make the best of every situation for His glory. We can pray for endurance and wisdom to run our races well. We will all face difficulties, but by God's grace, we will have blessings too. The pain will be wrapped in joy. The sorrow will be wrapped in incredible gifts.

Much like Joseph, we will have high highs, low lows, mundane days, and everything in between. But God is faithful to meet us where we are. Being obedient to the Lord will bring us joy. The Bible says, "Joyful are people of integrity, who follow the instructions of the LORD. Joyful are those who obey his laws and search for him with all their hearts. They do not compromise with evil, and they walk only in his paths" (Ps. 119:1–3).

> **Because I am a Christian, I assumed God would treat me differently and not allow as much suffering.... Our trials do not negate God's love for us.**

When my life seems hopeless and depressing, I long for the day when Jesus will make all things right. When life is heavy and painful, I can't wait to be with Him. But there is powerful hope and joy in remaining grateful for God's blessings even in the midst of suffering. Sometimes it helps to be reminded of the things that bring us joy. Things such as:

- breathing in crisp fresh air after a long run
- a good night's sleep
- holding your baby for the first time and thinking, *What did I do to deserve this perfect gift?*
- the thrill of planning a vacation, researching all the best locations and fun activities

- a fresh snow covering everything in a blanket of peace and cold stillness
- that first sip of hot coffee in the early morning
- watching the kids open presents in their pajamas on Christmas morning
- buying fresh flowers for the kitchen table
- finding a friend who feels like a soul sister, someone who gets you
- a random date night with your spouse
- a new job offer you've been praying for
- receiving money for groceries just when you needed it
- finding out you're pregnant after trying for years
- finding the perfect shoes that happen to be on sale
- smelling a homemade meal from a friend
- witnessing the wonder of a sunrise
- waking up to kisses from your child who somehow ended up in your bed
- breathing deeply after a long day at work
- a clean house
- being out in nature
- sand between your toes and a sun-kissed nose
- a much-needed conversation with a friend
- freshly cleaned laundry and cozy blankets
- reading a good book or watching your favorite movie while the rain pours outside
- going to church and hearing from the Lord

- spending holidays with family
- cracking open a new journal
- freshly baked cookies
- singing in the car with the windows down

I could go on and on about the goodness of God and the blessings He lavishes on us. Everything we have is His, and yet He graciously invites us to experience life to the fullest with Him. Joy can be found every day if only we choose to look for it. Remember, "don't copy the behavior and customs of this world, but let God transform you into a new person by changing the way you think. Then you will learn to know God's will for you, which is good and pleasing and perfect" (Rom. 12:2).

We are so fortunate. God doesn't have to give us anything because He already gave everything: His Son. But He wants to show His love and affection, reminding us of His tender care. Life isn't always easy, but finding the small (and sometimes big) blessings mixed in with the hard is a practice that can keep us going. When we focus on these gifts and His promises, our joy will remain. Even in hard times—or maybe especially then—it's all about our perspective.

There will undoubtedly be times when we won't experience contentment and joy. You may be debilitated with grief, depressed because of difficult circumstances, or doubting the goodness of God. There are times when we hit rock bottom and have no desire to get back up. Loss and disease and relational issues and betrayal and trauma can leave us crying on earth and craving eternity.

But these are exactly the times when it's so powerful to choose joy and gratitude.

But for today, I'm grateful for the small things because they truly are the big things to hold on to in life.

Today, in this exact moment, while I have tired eyes, little energy, and my own set of trials, I thank God for the blessings around me. The new flowers blooming outside, a baby girl sleeping on my chest, a roof over my head, and the freedom to open a Bible and read it without persecution. I do not take any of these lightly. I do not deserve any of these gifts, and I know everything could change tomorrow. But for today, I'm grateful for the small things because they truly are the big things to hold on to in life.

reflections

Take Action

While it's hard to understand the blessing in every trial we face, how has the goodness of God been evident throughout your life? Take a few minutes to remember. Make a list—aloud or on paper—of all the things you are grateful for and all the ways God *has* come through.

Key Verse

> The LORD your God in your midst,
> The Mighty One, will save;
> He will rejoice over you with gladness,
> He will quiet you with His love,
> He will rejoice over you with singing. (Zeph. 3:17 NKJV)

Closing Prayer

Lord, I know there will be times when I don't understand Your plan. There have been times when I couldn't sense Your presence or see any beauty around me. In those moments, I ask You to meet me where I am and remind me of Your sovereignty. What a glorious future I have because of the cross. Help me to recognize all You *have* done instead of wishing my life were different. Give me the strength and wisdom to look past my hardships and focus on the good. Help me refocus and see Your good gifts every day. Whether that's hot coffee in the morning or a warm bed at night, I pray Your Spirit would shift my perspective and keep me walking in obedience.

rest in Jesus

Shocked, Stressed, and the Prize

Two weeks before we were due to move across the country to North Carolina and take on a new adventure as a family of five, my oldest son spotted something on my neck. Wesley was only four years old at the time, and we were playing "airplane." I was lying on my back with my legs up in the air, balancing his small body on my feet. I clutched his hands as he zoomed through the air.

Between flying and many belly laughs, my son looked at me and said, "What is that, Mommy?"

He had a puzzled look on his face as he pointed at me. I immediately thought it was a "zip" (what my kids call zits) or maybe a smudge of the chocolate I had snuck during naptime. I brushed quickly at my face with my hand.

"It's still there, on your neck," Wesley said.

Thankfully, Andrew was home and came over to take a look. In less than two weeks, he would be graduating from medical school. "Honey, that doesn't look normal. You need to get that checked out."

Everyone calm down. I'm fine, I thought.

I slowly walked over to the mirror. I was fine. There was maybe a little lump on the right side of my neck, no bigger than a Ping-Pong ball. I probably just needed some thyroid medication. It was a little odd that I had never noticed it before. Then again, I don't have time to put on makeup in the morning, let alone check myself out in the mirror.

"I'll wait until we move and get settled in North Carolina to get this figured out."

The soon-to-be doctor in our household offered a second opinion. "No, you need to get an appointment *before* we move. Call now," Andrew said.

I didn't have time for this. I was packing an entire house while Andrew finished up his medical degree. We had birthday parties and goodbye parties and graduation parties and a million loose ends to tie up, all in the span of two weeks. But I did what my husband suggested and scheduled an appointment.

Fast-forward a few days, and I found myself in my car outside the doctor's office, sitting with the news of cancer. Cancer at thirty years old.

How can this be? I thought. *I'm healthy and young and busy and don't have time for this! My family needs me.*

I had just had a miscarriage, we were about to move far away from our friends and family, I had boxes covering every inch of my house, our new health insurance wouldn't start for another month, and now this.

Instead of my heart sinking, I came out guns blazing at first, with anger and questions and a "let's get this crap over with" attitude.

While my power-through personality has served me well at times, I finally shrank under the weight of the circumstances. God had given me more than I could handle … again.

Because I was already in a place of pain over my miscarriage and our move, I officially checked out when cancer became my new reality. The pain felt so personal, and the timing couldn't have been worse. Why couldn't God have waited to allow cancer until we were settled in our new home? Why couldn't He have allowed it years before when we didn't have kids? Why was this happening right when my husband was about to start residency? Andrew would be gone all the time. How was I going to care for the children while going through treatment? Why now?!

We all walk through hard things, of course, but this was all too much at one time. I kept hearing all the pat answers, such as "God will get you through" and "He will never give you more than you can handle." But He sure did!

He gave me *way* more than I could ever possibly handle. I nearly collapsed under the weight of it all. I felt God had forsaken me, pulled the rug out from under my feet. At the same time, I wanted to keep pushing through so cancer would be a distant memory. I wanted it all to be over. Cancer and surgery and treatment and our move and the bills and my husband's program and, and, and … I saw a mountain in front of me, and while I used to be able to sprint to the top of mountains, this was far too steep and I was far too weary. I didn't think I'd ever reach the top.

But maybe reaching the top wasn't the goal. Maybe my prize wasn't just being cancer-free or having my husband finish his residency. I needed to shift my focus and recognize that my sole purpose is to glorify God and know without a doubt that it is Jesus Himself who is the prize. I had been living as if being in perfect health with a perfect schedule and no problems was the ultimate goal, but it wasn't.

I was able to rest and pause with my Savior because there is no other end goal.

Once I started realizing this, I was able to sit awhile and experience the presence of the Lord. I was able to rest and pause with my Savior because there is no other end goal. I already have the prize—a relationship with Jesus. Suffering was making me more like Him. But getting to this place of joy, rest, and peace was quite the journey.

Questions and Surrender

I used to think I was "tight" with Jesus because He had allowed a lot of hardships in my life. Maybe He entrusted me with a lot of difficult circumstances because He knew I could handle them. Maybe I was one of His favorites because I was strong and could get through anything. While those statements couldn't be further from the truth, walking through cancer took both my distorted view of God and my relationship with Him to a whole new level. Any ounce of joy I had left at that point fled, and I began questioning God.

Of course, as a Christian, I knew everything in life was for God's glory. I kept telling myself the cancer would bring Him glory too, but my questions kept me from believing that. What was the point of being here on earth if my life would be filled with so much pain and heartache that I could barely survive? I looked at others around me and felt so alone, as if I were the only one dealing with so many hardships.

I remember accusing God, "After everything You've already allowed in my life, how could You let me get cancer?"

My sweet husband was the rock of our family the year I went through cancer. He put everyone else's needs before his own, and I could brag about him for days, but it was his answer to that question that had the greatest impact on me.

Andrew told me, "If you don't question His blessings, why do you question your suffering?"

That made me pause and think about my pain and God's sovereignty in a different way. God used my husband to break a belief I'd had for years. When God brings a timely blessing into my life, I don't respond by questioning, "Why did You do this for me, God? Why on earth did You allow this?" Everything I have is an undeserved gift from God.

But when something bad came my way, I questioned God's faithfulness and goodness instead of continuing to have an attitude of praise, solidified in joy. I needed to remind myself that He would use all the hard things I will ever go through to draw me to Himself. God is not the one to blame for our suffering.

I slowly started to realize how important it was for me to sit with the pain instead of trying to push through it. I was beginning to learn that this tendency sometimes kept me from experiencing joy too. While I was used to powering through the pain, I knew the only way to get through cancer was if I took the back seat and let God drive. I had many foundational questions concerning my faith that I needed to process with the Lord. Some of my honest questions were:

- *Why does it feel like I'm the only one going through hardships? Why me?*
- *Are we created just to live a life of pain?*
- *Shouldn't Christians experience less suffering than non-Christians? And if not, why?*
- *Are God's timing and plan really better than mine?*
- *If I die, will that really bring God the most glory?*
- *What if I stay sick and have a body full of cancer?*
- *If I can't be a good mom right now, what is my purpose?*

Nothing was making sense to me. These questions swirled in my mind, and I struggled not to feel completely worthless.

The year that followed my diagnosis consisted of various grueling treatments. We began with a surgery to remove the tumor in my neck, my thyroid, and the rest of the cancer in my body. As I walked the hospital halls with my husband, I was surrounded by other cancer patients who were mostly decades older than me, and I felt so out of place.

Then came the radioactive iodine treatment to kill the rest of the cancer in my body. I had to be confined to my room for over a week, eat a special diet for a month, and avoid every living thing for a week (plants included). The doctors said my body had so much radioactivity that I could set off airport security alarms. Clearly, I couldn't be around my kids, which was devastating.

Finally, I started having regular scans, neck ultrasounds, and monthly blood work to find the perfect dosage of medication that I'd be on for the rest of my life. No natural healing or oil could fix this. I would have to take thyroid medication every morning in order to survive. Would I ever feel "normal" or like myself again?

I didn't want to be weak or to be seen as needy. I wanted my life to reflect the strength and joy of the Lord … but sometimes strength means surrender.

With a husband in residency, three small boys, and no family nearby, it's a wonder we even got through. I wanted to be strong and courageous. I wanted to be alive and thriving. I wanted to be productive and impactful. But at what cost? Until I learned to quiet my spirit, take a deep breath, and rest in the Lord, I wouldn't find lasting joy in my trials.

Another beautiful thing about resting in the Lord is that you're able to see other people walk in their strengths. The focus shifts from *your agenda* to *the Lord's agenda*. When you take the back seat, you become a receiver, the one who is served rather than a doer. My whole life I'd been a doer, but this new challenge forced me to let others serve me.

I saw so many people step in to be the hands and feet of Jesus. I saw their authentic love and service poured out over our family when I was too helpless to give them anything in return. They didn't care how productive I could be, how great of a mom I was, or how I could repay them for their help. This season wasn't about how much I could accomplish or how fast I could unpack our house. It was quite the opposite. It was about sitting back and letting God work. For far too long I had equated inactivity with laziness, but I was learning there are times to run and times to rest. This was a time of rest for me. For the first time in my life, I discovered the pause button when I thought only the play and fast-forward buttons existed.

When I paused, I also saw my husband in a completely different way. He willingly emptied and cleaned my neck drains, wiped me after I went to the restroom, and washed my hair for me. I'm sure he didn't expect to have to do any of that until we were at least ninety years old. Even as he excelled in his residency program, he was focusing on his family. During that season, he was mom, dad, provider, homemaker, supporter, cook, and everything else in between. It still brings me to tears when I remember how he demonstrated his deep love for me. I am so grateful.

Ultimately, choosing to rest in Jesus brought me peace. In Him, I was able to live out this powerful truth: "In repentance and rest is your salvation, in quietness and trust is your strength" (Isa. 30:15 NIV). I was so helpless, but that enabled me to reflect on what God was doing and really listen. That's not to say it wasn't hard. Being confined to a private room during treatment and sitting with my thoughts was painful. I came out stronger, so of course God was gracious to use it. But I spent several months processing and wrestling with heavy questions about God and Christianity, which was a painful process.

I journaled the following a few weeks after surgery:

> Cancer is controlling me, and I want to figure out
> how I can control it. I'm depressed, I'm searching for

joy as I put on a smile, and I want to be in some type of control over my life because I feel so helpless.... Honestly, I thought cancer would make me stronger, a better mom, or appreciate my life more. I thought cancer would help me become slow to anger or have a quieter spirit. But honestly, none of that is happening. So what are You doing, God? What's Your big plan for my life? Is this it? Is this the new me? Tired all the time, depressed, hopeless, and stagnant? How am I supposed to thrive as a mom and wife? What am I supposed to offer the world?

Then a month later, I wrote:

There are seasons to be still and seasons to be warriors. Seasons to rest and seasons to run the race. We can't skip over pain.

In that first entry you get a glimpse of the angry, raw Nicole. I couldn't see past my misery and painful physical condition. I had to ask the hard questions and sift through the pain. I had to pause and go before the Lord with my most authentic self. I had to get to a place of understanding how suffering brings me closer to Christ, even when it felt like it was making me resent Him.

God is not afraid of your questions or doubts, friends. He's not surprised by how difficult it is for us to understand why we endure certain trials. He's not shocked when we're in over our heads. His ways are not our ways.

Reflecting made me ask the hard questions about life on earth as well. What does life mean? Why create people just to make us endure suffering? I didn't *feel* significant while confined to a bed and unable to do anything, but I had to look at the bigger picture. If you have a heartbeat, God is not done with you, even if it *feels* like it's over. I'm so glad I didn't give up, and I'm so glad God didn't give up on me.

> **If you have a heartbeat, God**
> **is not done with you, even**
> **if it *feels* like it's over.**

Embracing the stillness helped me surrender my life to God. I was no longer in control of my life. As much as I thought I'd surrendered to the Lord in the past, cancer was a whole other ball game. My resentment turned to appreciation. God was walking with me through the pain. And no matter what happened, I had hope for an eternity with Him where there would be no more tears or mourning. And I found joy in recognizing the blessings around me in spite of my circumstances.

The Promise of Stillness

Actually settling into rest and stillness during difficulties is easier said than done. Nothing in me wants to wallow in the muck, so it's tempting to ignore my feelings and move on. But I see now that there is a large amount of time and space between resting and moving on.

I thought pausing to rest equaled wallowing and having a pity party, but that isn't the case.

Maybe you're good at resting in the Lord. Maybe you're good at letting God slow you down so you have time to reflect. Maybe you're able to sit in the darkness while knowing there is hope, and if so, that is amazing. I want to be more like that.

But for those of us who are afraid to feel the pain, who see no light at the end of the tunnel, or who don't feel God's closeness, rest must become a learned practice.

Here are some practical things I now do instead of rushing on to the next thing when I know my heart, head, and spirit need to pause:

1. Pause
Be still. Don't make a quick decision. Don't rush or jump ahead. Commit to sitting with the pain, which can be extremely uncomfortable. Sometimes it's in that uncomfortable spot that we grow the most.

2. Be Present
The first thing I want to do when pain comes is skip ahead to the next season. I don't want to deal with it or focus on it. But I've found that if I live in the moment, ordinary moments sustain me: a kid's birthday, a hair appointment, doing laundry, making dinner. When you walk slowly and intentionally and concentrate on these everyday gifts, you will feel God's presence.

3. Write It Down

I'm a big fan of journaling. Writing things down always helps me process what is happening and what I'm feeling.

4. Talk It Out

Talking to a spouse, close friend, or counselor can be life-giving. But most of all, talk with God. Share your feelings and questions and doubts.

I wish I could have snapped my fingers and removed the physical pain. I wish I could have moved on to the next trial because this one hurt so deeply. I bet Jesus wished He could have done the same. Knowing what was to come, I bet He wished His Father would have mustered up another plan for Him, one that might not be so difficult or full of excruciating pain (see Matt. 26:39).

Here's the truth, though, friends: we will continue to walk through hard things. It's what we do with life's challenges that determines our growth. When we are in step with the Spirit, we'll know when it's time to pick up our mats or when it's time to sit down and grieve. We will have great days and hard days. We will have mountains and valleys. But learning when to run and when to rest will determine whether we have joy in all seasons.

And for those wondering how long is too long to rest, I think it's a personal decision between you and God. You know if you're sitting in your negativity longer than you need to, and you know in the back of your mind if you're shoving the pain aside. Pray for the wisdom to navigate both the highs and the lows of each season.

As of today, I am healthy with "no sign of disease." Sometimes that's all I can hold on to when I'm nearing a scan or not feeling my best. But when I live by the Lord's agenda and not my own, I will find rest in Him no matter what comes my way. "I wait quietly before God, for my victory comes from him. He alone is my rock and my salvation, my fortress where I will never be shaken" (Ps. 62:1–2).

As I reflect on the season of fighting cancer, you know what I see? I see that God never left me. He was with me the day I was diagnosed. He was with me as I writhed in pain after surgery. He was with me during isolation despite my dark doubts. He was with me as I sorted out my faith. If you think about it long enough, you'll notice He's been there through every awful event of your life. He will be with you through every blessing and the deepest pain you'll face. He is close.

Choosing rest made me see God's sovereignty and love because He didn't *have* to help me through. But He did anyway. I could have stayed in my depression and doubts. I could have kept sulking in my room and stayed angry at Him. I could have held on to the pain. But "by his wounds we are healed" (Isa. 53:5 NIV). By His grace He got me through.

You might be thinking, *But I'm not strong enough, Nicole!* I get it. If you'd told me years ago that cancer would be a part of my life at such a young age, I wouldn't have thought I'd ever be strong enough or close enough to God to get through. That's the point, though! Hardship and suffering demonstrate that though we are weak, He is strong. His power is made perfect in our weakness (see 2 Cor. 12:9 NIV). When we walk through hard things, we have to rely on Him and surrender. He wants our whole hearts, and He deserves them.

It took major time, prayer, and surrender on my part, realizing I am nothing without His grace, but God sustained me. It was cancer that made me never want to forget the truth that I still need Him in every moment. Even on the good days.

Nothing fills us to the brim and brings more healing and peace than Jesus. But sometimes it takes reflection and rest to see what God is doing. I know the resting is hard, but we can't always power through pain. We might feel good moving on from a season of suffering without taking time to experience healing, but skipping this step will strip us of joy in the long run. Reflection and rest help us remember that we can face hard things and endure. I pray that through the process of pausing and reflecting, we will learn, rest, grow, and restore our joy.

reflections

Take Action

Take some time to sit and rest at the feet of Jesus. If you only power through your pain, you're going to find yourself weary and maxed out. Rest in Jesus and allow Him to fill your cup and quiet you with His strength and love.

Key Verse

"I wait quietly before God, for my victory comes from him. He alone is my rock and my salvation, my fortress where I will never be shaken." (Ps. 62:1–2)

Closing Prayer

Lord, I so desperately do not want to sit in this place of pain. I want to move on, but I know there is a purpose in rest. In the same way You rested after creating the world, help me to take time to pause and reflect on what You've done and who You are. I pray that You would give me fresh energy and make me more like You through the process. I trust that I can glorify You in all things, whether I'm running my race with perseverance or sitting quietly and working out my salvation. Show me when I need to make time for rest and seek Your peace.

take responsibility

Big-Girl Pants

It was an unusually hot day in September, and I felt awful. My medications were off, I was still healing from surgery and cancer treatment, my husband was in the throes of residency, we were far from our friends and family, and all I wanted to do was lie around in bed. My depression was the worst it had ever been.

Do you ever have those days—or weeks or years—when life feels so overwhelming that you don't even know how to take a first step? Or you're so depressed that you think the darkness will be there forever? That's where I was.

My three rowdy boys were only five, three, and one, and life wasn't going to stop, no matter how much I wanted it to—even needed it to—at times. The two oldest boys came into my room that morning with big smiles and loud voices. They definitely wouldn't be happy if I was lying in bed all day. And they wouldn't survive without their momma. I rolled out of bed and tried to find my glasses so I could get going. I needed to make them breakfast, pack them snacks, and make sure the house was clean. They needed me to take them to preschool and to the store to buy baseball shoes. I had a day full of errands and appointments and a T-ball game that night. I slipped on some sweatpants as the boys ran around the house in just their undies while I rummaged in their rooms for some clean clothes.

If you have young kids, you know they have more energy than everyone else in the house combined. My boys get dirty regardless of what they're doing, they quickly switch from one activity to the next, and they're not fans of sitting still. Because of that, we are all about toy car races, superheroes, crafts, obstacle courses, and fun in our home. There is much love, many tight hugs, and lots of slobbery kisses when you're a mom, and there's nothing I'd rather be. But it's exhausting. And it's okay to acknowledge that.

While I needed a break, I wanted to make up for lost time, since I had been intermittently absent during surgery and treatment. My energy was still limited, and each day was draining me. I felt like I couldn't live up to the "fun mom" title I had assigned myself. I couldn't keep up.

So there I was—weighed down, feeling low, barely holding my own life and health together every morning—and yet I still had a million responsibilities. I was still their mother and I was still a wife. I still had kids to love and groceries to buy and a house to run and a family I was responsible for. Even in the moments when I wished away the physical and emotional pain and hoped for a day when I'd be feeling better and out from under this dark cloud, I knew my family depended on me.

In fact, it was (and still is) the decision to take responsibility for my family that ultimately and gradually brought me out of depression and helped me recapture a joyful life.

First Corinthians 4:20 reads, "The Kingdom of God is not just a lot of talk; it is living by God's power." What I've learned is that we can talk about how rough we have it, we can sit in our pain for a long time, and we can sulk under the weight of our circumstances, but it isn't until we *practice* what we preach that joy comes. On the other hand, we can talk about grace, restoration, and God's power, but it's just a bunch of talk until we actually live it out. Our responsibility is not to a religion but rather to living out a renewed life in Christ. It's more than just head knowledge; it's about having humility and understanding the undeserved grace that God has given us. Our joy flows from this heart connection.

This process reminds me of the moment in *The Pilgrim's Progress* when Christian and Faithful are discussing matters of living out their faith and what they've observed in others. "We find talkative fools that can only speak about faith and whose hearts are morally corrupt and proud. Their claim to faith confuses the world, places a stain on Christianity, and grieves those that are sincere in their faith."[1]

God was giving me an opportunity to live out my faith and make it more than just words, as an example for those around me, especially my family. He was allowing me opportunity after opportunity to put into practice what I believed so that my struggles would be turned into responsibility, which in turn would cause a heart change and sincere faith.

There comes a time when our words and beliefs without actions are meaningless. There comes a time when we must take responsibility for the life—the people—entrusted to us. Not ignoring or avoiding our pain but working for the Lord in the midst of it.

Colossians 3:23 came to mind when I was battling depression: "Whatever you do, work at it with all your heart, as working for the Lord" (NIV). God made me a mother and a wife, and those responsibilities don't just go away because I'm not *feeling* it. While valid, feelings don't represent the full truth of any situation. Even though I was depressed, I still had to fulfill my role as a mom and a wife. It was time to move past reflection and toward owning my circumstances. I knew that if I abdicated my role as wife and mom, I'd quickly be back in a dark trench surrounded by piles of laundry and unhappy children.

> **While valid, feelings don't represent the full truth of any situation.**

But more than that, I had the gift of young children to love. I had a husband who poured so much into our marriage and family while I was going through cancer that, even though I was still healing, I knew it was time for me to pitch in. If we continue to make life about us, then we'll never know when to stop. It was time for me to switch gears, move forward, and offer my best.

Now don't hear me saying we need to push ourselves so hard that we end up with severe depression, get sick, or wind up angry at everyone. However, working for the Lord means giving our best. And everyone's best is different because we are individuals, "fearfully and wonderfully made" (Ps. 139:14 NIV). I knew my work for the Lord would not be in vain, even if I had to force myself to get out of bed. Sometimes we don't *feel* like doing much, but we owe it to the people around us to put on our big-girl pants and take responsibility. We can't just check out.

I think that, in our culture today, we like to sit a little too long in our crap. We want to have a pity party that never ends or dwell on the hard stuff without pursuing healing and change. We feel that having challenges gives us a connection to others, something to talk about, and a way to sympathize with others' weaknesses. But where is the strength in staying in the mess? Where is the determination and gumption and grit? Where was the fighter I knew I always had been?

Jesus came so we could live abundant lives in Him—full of Him, our hope in Him, our freedom in Him, our joy in Him—not so we could waste time as we sulk in our sorrows, day in and day out. I had to make a change.

I understand that there are times when you hit rock bottom and it is only through the power of the Holy Spirit that you can get back up. I understand that when you are going through severe depression, you can't just snap out of it and move on. I understand that there is a season for healing and grief and that restoration takes time.

In my own story, with every school drop-off, every meal made, every cleaning day, every story read before bedtime, and every pile of clean laundry folded, God used my responsibility to my family to slowly pull me out of my depression. There is joy in service, and God sometimes uses our obligations. Whether it is our children, work, or community, there are times when serving others can keep us moving forward through trials. And ultimately, fulfilling our responsibilities will bring us lasting joy.

Overcoming Depression and Darkness

While it seems like I knew exactly what to do to get myself out of depression, I want you to know that was absolutely not the case. It wasn't an overnight fix or a one-time prayer. It wasn't a choice that I made one day or the result of one powerful encounter with the Holy Spirit. It wasn't one sermon or one worship song that set me straight. While I can look back and see how God got me through and how each of those things helped, I couldn't even see a glimmer of hope when I was living with depression. Depression makes you feel trapped in your own thoughts and pain. To be honest, there was no amount of Scripture reading, antidepressants, or shopping sprees that could bring me back.

I felt isolated, as if I were doing this "Christian" thing wrong again. If I loved Jesus and He was truly my strength, why did I need antidepressants? If I was truly saved, wouldn't Jesus be all that I needed? I felt a lot of shame because I couldn't break free on my own. I thought this was how it would always be, and I became weary of "trying" and not seeing a change.

Depression is debilitating, and sadly, I'd be lying if I said I've never asked the Lord to take my life and bring me home because I felt so low and worthless.

I remember lying in my hospital bed after the surgery to get rid of the cancer, struggling through the waves of pain, and I wanted to give up. I felt as if my once-athletic body was now as old and frail as a ninety-five-year-old woman's. This was not the life I wanted to live. As I lay there, I specifically remember saying, "God, I can't do this. Please take me home." My once-energetic personality that thrived in life felt like a distant memory. Who was that girl? It seemed as if she were gone for good after everything I had walked through. My fight was gone. I wanted my life to be over.

For years after I was raped, I worked to get to a place of trust with the Lord, to find true joy again. But then I felt completely smashed down again after my cancer diagnosis. The trials I had faced weren't building me up the way I wanted them to. Instead, I was getting weaker on the outside and angrier on the inside with each passing day. I wanted to be done.

In my misery, I doubted my Maker.

In my pain, I questioned my Source of peace.

In my darkness, I questioned my Defender.

In my weakness, I doubted my Way Maker.

Jesus, take me. I meant those words with my whole heart. There had been difficult times before when I wished for Jesus to make His grand return, but this was different. I couldn't move forward, and I had no desire to be on earth anymore.

Jesus, take me. Please take me.

I've never audibly heard God speak before or seen Him with my physical eyes, but in that moment, I felt a hand on mine and heard the Spirit whisper, "I'm not done with you."

That was all I needed.

In that moment, I knew that regardless of how frustrating the healing process would be, how awful I felt, how hard this was going to be on my family, or how stressed out I was over our medical bills, I needed to move forward out of obedience and hope. I clung to that word from God for months afterward and still do today, because I still have days of depression and pain and hopelessness. But God is not done with me, and He is absolutely not done with you.

> **You are valued by God, and He has a purpose tailored specifically for you. God's not done with you.**

If you've been in this dark place before, I am so sorry. If you're still in this place today as you read this, the only thing I can say is, keep going because God is not done with you. You still have breath in your lungs for a reason, and now more than ever, I know our days are numbered and He will call us home when it's our time.

But now is not that time. If you're reading this, you are alive. You might not feel amazing or be living your best life, but you are still here. If you find yourself losing hope or being overtaken by darkness, reach out to a trusted friend or family member that you can share honestly with. You are valued by God, and He has a purpose tailored specifically for you. God's not done with you.

So where do we go from here?

Seven Ways to Take Responsibility

The definition of *responsible* is "answerable or accountable, as for something within one's power, control, or management."[2] When it comes to working through depression, taking responsibility means we take ownership over our own lives as best we can. It means we work with what we have and continue to move forward, one small step at a time. Yes, coming out of depression is a work of the Spirit, and in some cases, He works in a split second and takes that depression away. But for most of us, I'm guessing it's a battle we continue to face. But let's not live there and let's absolutely not end there.

A wide range of severity exists when it comes to depression, and everyone is on his or her own journey. Therefore, there is no one-size-fits-all solution, nor are there guaranteed strategies that will always work for the majority of people. But here are a few ways I've taken responsibility over my own life when it comes to my mental health.

1. Become More Selfless

One of the biggest things I've learned in my Christian walk is that life is not all about me. Ouch. Not exactly something I want to hear when I'm depressed. But when I grasped the seriousness of my responsibility to my family, my selfishness started to dwindle and my joy slowly returned over time.

2. Turn Understanding into Action

I've heard it said before that the evidence of real faith is a transformed life. That doesn't mean dismissing the pain but that I'm moving forward rather than staying stuck. When I began showing up for my family, going to work, and being involved in my community, my focus shifted. I still struggled with depression at times (and still do today), but it slowly became a distant emotion when my actions followed my beliefs.

3. Laugh Often and See the Big Picture

It might feel unthinkable in the moment, but when I watched a show that made me laugh or I had a lighthearted conversation with a friend, everything else felt lighter. I cranked up the music in my kitchen and danced with my kids. Or I showered and got ready and went out to dinner. I *chose* to get out of bed. I decided not to let depression be the end of my story.

4. Notice the Beauty around Me

Beauty can pull us up out of our struggles. Whether it was watching a lovely sunset, being thankful for my marriage, taking a few quiet moments in the morning to read in peace, watching my children play, or seeing God's overarching story of grace in my life, being intentional about noticing these moments helped. Whether big or small, recognizing the beauty and blessings God provides brought me through the pain. We can have hope and joy in the Lord because of our secure future, where we will have no more pain or suffering.

5. Find Activities That Bring Me Peace

I was recently talking with a friend who loves to paint when she's anxious. Each of us has a hobby or activity that calms us down or breathes life back into our souls. Maybe for you it's music or crafting or working out. All these practices can be done for the glory of God and as acts of worship. Dig deep and find those things that restore your joy. For me it's baking, doing something creative, cleaning, being outside, and making time to fellowship with friends and family even when I'm tempted to isolate myself.

6. Live in the Moment

Thinking too far ahead left me with more anxiety and depression. When I instead chose to breathe deeply, focus on the here and now, and live in the moment, I saw things for what they were. I could be thankful even when my circumstances weren't ideal.

7. Embrace Therapeutic Approaches

For me, part of taking responsibility for my depression was to not silently suffer. Playing the martyr never got me anywhere. I shared with my husband how horrible my mental health was, and I sought help from a Christian counselor. I even went on medication for a time. I did what needed to be done to ensure I could fulfill my obligations to myself and my family. Pray about what you need to do, and then just do it.

These strategies helped me when I was going through depression, but they can be valuable no matter what struggle you're facing. Because when it comes down to it, if we are honest with ourselves, there will always be something that can ruin our day, week, month, or year. I can always find something to get worked up about. It's tempting to hold on to the pain of my past or become mired in bad habits. But part of trusting God is not getting stuck in your emotions.

As I mentioned in the first chapter, I found it easy to follow my heart or do what *felt* right. I had been led by emotions rather than living a life of spiritual discipline full of faithfulness, obedience, and responsibility. I lived a life of integrity and was always held to a high standard at school, sports, and church, so it was *easy* to do the right thing. But when I lost my health and support system and battled depression while raising three small kids virtually alone, feelings were no longer enough to keep me going.

This is why I'm such a firm believer in the idea that allowing God to use you where you are can lift you out of the trenches. As we take responsibility for our actions, words, and life and stop blaming others or God for our circumstances, we will find joy and freedom. But if we continue down a path of negativity and wallowing, unwilling to change, not being honest with ourselves or others, let alone God, we're going to continue to live in a cycle of depression. How can we find relief if we don't make an effort to help ourselves or those around us? Remember, you were created for a purpose. As God's child, you have dignity and were bought with a price. Therefore, you have much to live for and your work isn't over.

Our main goal is to point others toward Jesus, not ourselves. Let's be women who share our testimony about what God has done. We need:

- More women who focus on present joys and aren't bound by their pasts
- More women who glorify the Lord instead of stealing attention for themselves
- More women who choose healing instead of staying stuck in their pain
- More women who share their faith with boldness without making it about themselves
- More women who walk in obedience, even when it's hard

- More women who take responsibility for their actions, words, and circumstances and stop blaming others
- More women who are warriors, who refuse to play the victim, who decide their battle ends now and won't back down

The time is now to know why you believe what you believe and walk it out wholeheartedly. And it starts in the home and in the workplace. It starts with the people around you—your friends and family and coworkers. Where can you be faithful today? Where can you take responsibility today?

A Greater Reward

One of the things I love about Paul is that regardless of his horrible past persecuting Christians, he took responsibility, repented, and moved forward with what Jesus was calling him to do. At one time, he was completely deceived. But when the Lord opened his eyes, he turned from his former ways and started living for God (see Acts 9).

Paul could have been so depressed about his previous behavior. He could have wallowed in his sin and shame, allowing his past to prevent him from fulfilling his purpose. Instead, he walked with the Lord. He followed Him. He acted. He listened. He spoke. He was moved by the Spirit. He did the next right thing. He put one foot in front of the other. He took responsibility. And look how much *joy* the Lord brought to his life. More than that, look at the *joy* he was to others because of his obedience.

I want to live like that—with intention and purpose. Repenting of my sins, knowing I need a Savior, but walking in step with the Spirit.

Part of taking responsibility is being consistent rather than doing what's convenient. We need to choose wisely. We find a great example of this in *The Pilgrim's Progress*. When Christian was climbing the Hill of Difficulty, he said, "I might become weak or even scared, but I will have courage and press on because it's better to be on the right path, even if it's difficult, than to go an easier way that ends in misery."[3]

Part of taking responsibility is being consistent rather than doing what's convenient.

In a similar way, fighting your way out and doing the right thing has a far greater reward than taking the easy path. During cancer and my depression, it was so easy to cry and sit in bed. It was easy to be self-focused and obsessed with my circumstances. When things are difficult, it's easy to make life about ourselves, take things personally, and find ways to live that don't require a heart change.

I pray that we remember our place at the foot of the cross. We were dead in our sins before Christ. And now, in Him, we are new creations and have new life. It's no longer about us, but about Him. I pray that regardless of the trials we face, we choose to take responsibility for the life we've been given.

That's hard to hear when you've lost your zest for life. It's hard to hear when life throws too much your way or when you see no end to hardship. But be encouraged, because God allows these obligations in our paths to help pull us out of the darkest trenches. While some of us need to take slower steps, I pray that we can all be women of obedience, faithfulness, and responsibility as we walk forward in grace and joy.

reflections

Take Action

Where in your life can you take more responsibility? We can wallow for only so long before it becomes a habit. Today, make one small change that propels you in the right direction. Others are counting on you.

Key Verse

"Whatever you do, work at it with all your heart, as working for the Lord." (Col. 3:23 NIV)

Closing Prayer

Lord, I'm so sorry for how I make life about myself at times. I know I'm here to glorify You and only You. I want my life to be a fragrant offering to You so those around me will know You. As I look around, I pray that You would show me what to do, how to act, who to reach out to, and where to take responsibility. Help me walk in obedience to You even when it's hard. Help me be faithful and endure even when it feels impossible. I don't want to play the victim or wallow, so instead, I choose to get up and let You lead me forward in victory.

stop complaining

Gas Station Water Bottles

Sometimes I struggle in my role as a mother. There are many moments when I can't believe God has blessed me with four sweet and healthy children. I look at my kids and think, *How in the world did I get so lucky?* I scroll through photos of them on my phone late into the night, watching videos of when they started walking. On their birthdays, I get emotional and wish time would just stand still. I love my kids with all my heart.

Then there are other days when I've had enough of everyone's whining, incessant questions, and bad attitudes. I don't want anyone touching me, I want to escape to an island all by myself, and I want to take a shower. A nice, long, hot shower with no reason to rush.

One morning, I yelled down the stairs at my three boys to grab all their school stuff before we rushed out of the house. I decided I had everything I needed. Keys, coffee, wallet. Done.

"Mom, I need help zipping my jacket up!"

"I don't know where my other shoe is!"

"Did you get our snacks, Mom?"

Of course, I hadn't had time to get ready for the day before school drop-off. Like many moms, I'm always the last one to brush my teeth and put on normal clothes. We always make sure the kids are taken care of first.

As I was buckling the kids into their car seats, my seven-months-pregnant belly (at the time) got in the way and forced me to look down. Shoot! I had forgotten to change shirts, and I still had my pajamas on, which meant about four inches of my bare belly was showing.

We couldn't be late, so there was no time for changing. I thought, *Oh well, I'll just shower and get ready when I get back home.* And we were off.

All was well in the car. We recited the kids' Bible memory verses while music played softly over the car speakers, and my mind drifted to all the emails sitting in my inbox. While the morning was some-what frantic, we were okay.

About ten minutes after leaving the house, Wesley, my oldest, suddenly realized we had forgotten their water bottles.

I don't know why it was such a big deal, but all three boys broke out into hysterical tears like I'd just run over their precious toys with the vacuum or something. (Which I may or may not have done before. On accident, of course.)

"I'm going to be so thirsty!"

"What? We can't drink any water today?"

"Mom, you have to turn around!"

More sobbing, more dramatic statements.

I told the boys that their classrooms probably had some water cups for them to use and that everything would be all right. But with each mile we drove, the complaining and tears kept coming.

I couldn't handle it, and I couldn't turn back, so I got off at the next exit to stop at a gas station. I'm sure I was a sight to see, with my belly hanging out, missing a certain undergarment, my hair a mess, and rocking my college sweatpants. I ordered those water bottles as fast as I could and checked out.

I turned to my kids and said, "Here! Are you happy now?"

Thankfully, the boys thought those gas station water bottles were the coolest things they'd ever seen. I sacrificed my image so they could be happy, but what's new?

All was well until my low-gas indicator flashed, followed by a bright check engine light. I dropped off my oldest but still had to drive clear across town to get my youngest two boys to preschool.

Usually I'm the type of person who fills up my gas tank when it's half-empty. I like to arrive early to events, and I plan out my weeks so that I have what I need to get through my long days with no help—at that time with three kids, and a baby on the way. I don't have the luxury of anyone else taking care of these details.

So there I was without a bra or a proper shirt, and now I was almost out of gas as well. What a winner.

I made it to yet another gas station just in time, then rushed the other two kids to school. My youngest may have screamed a little when I left the preschool, but I headed home alone, looking forward to taking a deep breath.

I took a quick shower, started some laundry, cleaned up the kitchen, and sat down to work on a few projects.

But then, instead of feeling grateful for a couple of hours to myself, I started thinking of all that I was lacking.

If only I had family close by, life would be so much easier.

If only my husband worked a nine-to-five job, I'd be happy.

I wish we had the finances for all the kids to be in the best schools.

I wish we could buy a more reliable car.

Instead of taking some time to be in the Word, I was just whining to God. The floodgates of complaining opened wide, and I started to feel angry about the seemingly never-ending tasks that consumed my days.

When am I ever going to be able to focus on what I want?

When will I finally have some help from my husband so I don't have to be a single parent?

These thoughts began to coalesce into an overwhelming feeling of dissatisfaction and despair. I needed to vent. I reached out to a few friends and talked with my mom. Before I knew it, my complaining spirit had spilled over into a full-blown pity party, and I struggled to pull myself out of the hole.

Then I remembered that Andrew was going to be home for dinner that evening. I needed to snap out of it in time to make a nice meal so we could spend some time together as a family. I wanted to take advantage of every moment we could have with him. While I was still annoyed that complaints had hijacked my morning, I was determined to make the next half of the day better than the first.

School pickup, lunch, and naps came and went. It was almost time for Andrew to come home. Dinner was ready, the kids were excited to see him, and I had even put on makeup and picked up the house. I felt great. Between wiping bottoms and breaking up fights, I gazed at the clock and realized it was already past six.

Ugh. When is he coming?

After a brief text exchange, I learned he wasn't going to make it home for dinner. A handful of patients had checked in last minute, and he had to stay to take care of them.

Instead of being supportive and understanding, I went full-on Miss Whiny Pants ... again:

He's never home!

All this was for nothing!

He clearly doesn't know how important this was to me or he'd be here.

We had a plan!

I was so angry. More than that, I felt hurt and disappointed. I hated my situation. I married my best friend for a reason, and I wanted to live life with him. Of course, I wanted him to have a great career, but I also didn't want to do everything alone, especially raising kids. I felt personally slighted and began questioning everything. *Why do all my friends have husbands who come home at a decent hour to eat dinner with the kids and help with the bedtime routine? Why am I the only one at basketball games, doing bath time, and making every meal every day?*

Why me, God?

Ugh. Just writing out my honest feelings from that day clearly exposes how much I need Jesus. Who was this insecure and angry girl?

The Consequences of Complaining

As a stay-at-home mom, sometimes I feel like the heartbeat of the family because of the role I play in setting the tone. I influence the emotions, communication, love, and even the volume in our home (our kitchen dance parties can be a little loud at times). Having this responsibility in our family keeps me accountable because I have four little kids constantly watching me. If I project my bad day onto them, guess who will also be difficult and have an attitude the rest of the day? Everyone! Dealing with one kid who is having a bad day can be overwhelming in and of itself, but all four? It's just not worth it.

Whether or not you're a parent, personal hardships, pain, and disappointment can lead you into the habit of complaining. Like any habit, it becomes easier and easier to complain the more you do it. The temptation to dwell on our suffering is often difficult to ignore. Additionally, I feel that my complaining is amplified when I face hardships alone. Over the last several years, I've started to notice that my complaining has had negative consequences in my life.

For starters, my complaining gave my kids permission to whine too. Kids love to mimic Mom and Dad. Sometimes it's cute when they repeat one of your funny sayings. But when they copy your bad behavior, they showcase your weaknesses and lack of maturity. As parents, we are called to encourage, uplift, and gently lead our children as we follow Christ. Whether we're parents or not, God calls us to lift others up, and this becomes a tall order when we're complaining and focused on ourselves.

Complaining always puts me in a worse mood. It robs me of any joy I have and makes me hard to be around. My complaints keep me stuck in a self-centered world where I become fixated on things that don't truly matter. There is nothing wrong with expressing grief or disappointment during hard times, but I need to ask myself what is worth complaining about and what isn't.

Optimism usually doesn't come naturally when inconveniences or hardship come our way. We've all selfishly complained about one thing or another, sulking or pasting on fake smiles so others will feel bad for us. It's easier to mope than it is to be positive when challenges hit you in the face. Think about it: it takes hard work and emotional effort to get out of a rut. Complaining does nothing for you or the people around you. It's not edifying, and it doesn't leave you feeling satisfied.

Negativity overpowers positivity like somebody wearing too much cologne or perfume on an airplane. No one likes that. Negative attitudes are also toxic and can lead to poor health, chronic stress, and even more rapid aging.[1] I've found this to be true in my own life. When the complaining seeps in, it envelops every aspect of my day. I grab unhealthy snacks out of the pantry as I'm rushing around, hoping a bite of something sweet will help. I become frazzled and stressed, my mind bombarded by negative thoughts instead of feeling calm and positive. If a simple change of attitude can truly turn around the toxic negativity, then I need to choose that every time.

Is It Ever Okay to Complain?

Life is filled with relatively petty inconveniences and hopefully rare traumatic events. Even though these are easy to distinguish from each other, we don't always act like it. Deep down in our hearts, we know what is unimportant and what is serious. We know the difference between selfish complaining and trusting God with every outcome.

For instance, I start complaining when:

- We're late for school … again!
- My kids are screaming and fighting.
- My husband is working eighty-plus hours a week and I'm exhausted.
- The dog chews on my outdoor furniture.
- I feel overwhelmed with my to-do list, with endless laundry and dishes and papers and homework.

None of these circumstances are a big deal on their own, but complaining can make each one seem like a much bigger deal. If all these things happen on the *same day*, then they can seem insurmountable. Our lives can truly be overwhelming in certain seasons, and there are times when all we want is for Jesus to come take us home. But what we don't want to do is let this sorrow or negativity become a pattern in our lives, which can easily happen.

When major trauma, depression, or a life-altering situation comes our way, it's normal to feel disappointed and sad. When you're going through something truly awful and you're expressing the difficulty in that, it's not called complaining anymore. The Bible has a word for it: *lamenting*. It's also how we ask for help—by sharing what we're going through. We've typically entered survival mode at this point, and we need supportive and loving people to surround us and help us through it. These deeper emotions aren't the same as giving in to complaints *in the moment* when you're feeling annoyed or forsaken.

I am personally trying to *choose* gratitude and praise God in my struggles instead of complaining. I tend to see things as black or white, so I used to think that if I wasn't complaining or angry, I had to be positive and happy all the time. I found it hard to live in the gray area in which I was hopeful some days and sad other days. Since I set the tone for my family, I figured I had better fake it to prove that Mommy had her act together. This didn't serve me well either. Being falsely positive in the face of ruined plans or loneliness felt ridiculous to me, like putting on a shirt that was seven sizes too big.

It's a choice to believe the best about God and believe His true motives are love and grace.

What I've learned is that it takes a lot of discipline to meditate on the truth so that complaining isn't my first reaction to trials. For me, this means concentrating on what God has done for me. As it says in Colossians 3:16, "Let the message of Christ dwell among you richly as you teach and admonish one another with all wisdom through psalms, hymns, and songs from the Spirit, singing to God with gratitude in your hearts" (NIV). It can feel like trials and complaining go hand in hand most of the time, but the truth is, our reaction is our *choice*. It's a choice to believe the best about God and believe His true motives are love and grace.

It's a choice to stop sulking.

It's a choice to ask God to make our words sweet and edifying to ourselves, our family, and others around us.

It's a choice to put ourselves aside and focus on others.

It's a choice to stand on the truth and live like we're saved and have the Holy Spirit dwelling inside us.

There will always be something we want, and there will always be someone who wants what we have. It's our choice to remain humble and thankful for what God has given us.

From Complaints to Thanks

One of the reasons we complain is because we feel that as Christians we are entitled to pain-free lives. Or we truly believe we deserve "better" lives. But that is so far from the truth. We are not promised easier lives because we love Jesus. Instead, Jesus Himself promised that our lives *would* be filled with hardships that point us to our true hope (see John 16:33).

But God will also be with us and provide peace, guidance, and joy every step of the way, hardships or not. We can know joy in trials, and we can praise Him instead of complaining to Him. The Bible is clear in instructing us to "consider it pure joy … whenever you face trials of many kinds, because you know that the testing of your faith produces perseverance" (James 1:2–3 NIV).

So much of my negativity and complaining were driven by fear and a bad attitude. But when I took a step back and looked around, I saw that so much in my life was good. I treasure my precious family even amid the chaos. When I felt my baby girl kicking inside my belly after walking through a miscarriage, I recognized that the miracle of life is such a special gift. I savor the safety of a home that's just the right size for us in this season. I look in the mirror and see that I'm healthy again after cancer. We have food on the table and warm clothes for when it's cold. My husband is a godly man who loves his family immensely. I know that everything he does is for us and our future.

You've probably seen those wooden signs that read "There's always something to be thankful for." As trite as that sentiment may seem in the midst of challenges, it's true. I have so much to be thankful for. We *all* have so much to be grateful for. Getting outside our own bubbles helps us to look at the world with fresh eyes and remember what God has done for us. Ultimately, we can find contentment in what the Lord has provided. When we fix our eyes on what we *do* have rather than on all the things we lack, we move from complaining to thanksgiving. When we try to take control in an attempt to remove the uncertainty from our lives, we don't leave room for God to provide and come through for us. (We'll explore this more in the next chapter.)

I am learning to trust that God has a good plan not for just my husband and kids but for *me* and my life as well. Remember, He cares deeply about each one of us, knows the intimate details of our lives, and is always orchestrating things for our good (see Rom. 8:28). It might not always feel like it, but we serve a loving God who wants what's best for us. He is working in our hearts to bring about our sanctification in Christ.

There's a story in Numbers 11 that illustrates God's response to selfish and complaining attitudes. As Moses led the Israelites during their forty years in the wilderness, they began to focus on their hardship rather than God's provision. "The people complained in the hearing of the LORD about their misfortunes, and when the LORD heard it, his anger was kindled, and the fire of the LORD burned among them and consumed some outlying parts of the camp" (v. 1 ESV).

God made His wrath felt when His people complained. The Israelites had been rescued from slavery in Egypt through God's miraculous intervention. God, because of His love for His people, made a way for them to be saved. He appointed Moses to lead the Israelites out of a terrible situation and fulfilled His promise. Yet here they were years later, yearning to go back into captivity because they wanted meat instead of being grateful for the fresh manna that God provided each day:

> The people of Israel also wept again and said, "Oh that we had meat to eat! We remember the fish we ate in Egypt that cost nothing, the cucumbers, the melons, the leeks, the onions, and the garlic. But now our strength is dried up, and there is nothing at all but this manna to look at." (vv. 4–6 ESV)

They sound like such whiners, don't they? But I'd been doing the exact same thing when I was complaining about my husband's schedule or my responsibilities as a mother, completely blinded to God's blessings and provision in my life. If we continue along this path of constant complaints without seeing the bigger picture, we will be robbed of true joy and peace. When life is rough, remember that God's grace and plans outweigh the hardships and inconveniences. We still have it good because of the God we serve. If only the Israelites had seen God's deliverance and provision clearly. If only they had remembered His gracious plan to rescue them from slavery, it would have saved them a lot of trouble.

If I tried to plan out my kids' lives, no matter how hard I tried, I could never plan them out more perfectly than God. I could envision great lives for them in which they'd never get hurt, always win, never fail, and achieve everything they ever dreamed. But in the end, you know what they'd turn out to be? Fearful, spoiled children who don't know what it's like to walk through pain, fall on their knees, and desperately need a Savior. If we don't experience trials, how else are we going to desire more of Christ and be refined to wholeness in Him?

When life is rough, remember that God's grace and plans outweigh the hardships and inconveniences.

Looking back, I recognize that complaining is a tactic the Enemy uses to keep us ungrateful and always wanting more. Satan doesn't want you to feel fulfilled by your manna; he wants you to always desire the meat and fancy food. Whatever keeps us content in Christ is what the Enemy will go after and try to steal (see John

10:10). Christ didn't just die for us, making a way for us to be with our heavenly Father for eternity, but He also gives us a chance each day to love and serve Him.

When there's an abundance of Jesus in our daily lives, there's an abundance of joy in our lives as a result. As Romans 5:3–5 says, "We rejoice in our sufferings, knowing that suffering produces endurance, and endurance produces character, and character produces hope, and hope does not put us to shame, because God's love has been poured into our hearts through the Holy Spirit who has been given to us" (ESV). A connection forms between our souls and His heart because of the sufferings, the disappointments, and even the annoyances we face.

Recently I heard the hymn "He Giveth More Grace" by Annie Johnson Flint. She was an orphan and dealt with rheumatoid arthritis, cancer, and a series of other major health issues that left her in excruciating pain. I vividly remember scrubbing the dishes with all my might and cranking up the volume. That day, exhaustion and depression had been getting the best of me. As I listened closely, I was inspired that Annie made the choice to see her trials as edification in Christ.

> He giveth more grace when the burdens grow greater,
> He sendeth more strength when the labors increase.

The hymn ends with the line "He giveth, and giveth, and giveth again." I encourage you to look up the rest of the lyrics. What a beautiful and joyful way of looking at our daily trials. When we view them as opportunities for God's provision and fulfillment and mercy, *we can stop asking why He allows certain things in our lives.*

God uses all the things we've had to endure to strengthen our relationship with Him. We've heard that a million times, but it never seems to feel true in the moment. We can be selfish, complain all day long, and doubt God's kindness because He's allowing us to endure so much, or we can humble ourselves and thank Him for giving us the opportunity to be used.

> ## God uses all the things we've had to endure to strengthen our relationship with Him.

I believe that people who know pain, experience great loss, or suffer much can see God come through for them in unique and powerful ways. The more burdens, the more grace. The more suffering, the more joy. Earthly pain and problematic situations provide opportunities to live out the gospel and experience the providence of God.

My prayer for you is that you'll be able to look back and see all that God did during hard seasons of your life and also that adopting an attitude of praise can get you out of the trench. Whether we face disappointments or the battle to stay positive when all seems lost, our mourning can truly be turned to dancing if we fix our eyes on God. It's not about faking our way through counseling or smiling when we're crying inside. When we are raw and authentic before the Lord and make the choice to give thanks in our trials instead of sulking and complaining, we will discover lasting joy and hope.

And, hey, if we keep a positive attitude and complain less, we might in fact live longer.

reflections

Take Action

Have you become trapped in a cycle of complaining? Identify two ways you will begin to change. When you find yourself going down that road today, pray that God would replace your complaints with praise and gratefulness.

Key Verse

"We also glory in our sufferings, because we know that suffering produces perseverance; perseverance, character; and character, hope. And hope does not put us to shame, because God's love has been poured out into our hearts through the Holy Spirit, who has been given to us." (Rom. 5:3-5 NIV)

Closing Prayer

Lord, thank You for my life. Despite the ups and downs, I thank You for giving me so many blessings. Help me to refocus my heart on things above, things that matter to You, so that I don't get caught in a cycle of complaining. Give me the strength to move past petty things quickly so that I can accomplish Your will. Help the words that come out of my mouth to be words of praise, not complaining. Everything I have is Yours. I commit this day to You and ask that my words would bring life, not death.

give up control

Dream House

It was Easter morning, and I couldn't shake my depression. I was so frustrated by my husband's work schedule. I was essentially a single parent. I never thought I'd be putting all the kids to bed by myself or attending meetings, baseball games, and school programs alone. I didn't know what our future held and was struggling to settle into our house because we might move again next year. The unending chaos and shifting plans seemed like too much for me and the kids. The weight of everything fell on me.

Easter was supposed to be a day of rejoicing. I was supposed to be thankful for the cross, humbled by Christ's sacrifice, and joyous that He is risen. Do you ever *know* the truth but it doesn't *feel* true? You're so caught up in your circumstances or pain that you can't see beyond it? That's exactly where I was on that Sunday morning.

I walked into my parents' backyard and found my grandma sitting on the patio, soaking up some sunshine. There wasn't a cloud in the sky. The birds were chirping, and my kids were running around the backyard, finding eggs and climbing trees while the baby slept inside. All seemed right with the world, yet my grandma and I were dealing with heavy hearts. We were both walking through difficulties that had us mourning on Easter, but we were also rejoicing *because* of Easter. We found ourselves stuck in the middle of joy and pain.

My grandma's walk with the Lord has spanned more than half a century, and she has faced things that no mother should ever have to experience. I often have a hard time heeding someone's advice if they haven't personally experienced something similar. But my grandma has faced so much suffering in her lifetime that anything she shares is practically gold to me. I knew she would be able to pour wisdom into my life that day. I sat down next to her and asked, "How do you do it, Grandma? How do you stay strong in your faith and trust God's plans when you keep walking through hard things?"

My grandma always spoke with such tenderness, and her words held the weight of enduring difficulty. She thought for a moment, then said, "Well, honey, you have to shift your thinking. Instead of dwelling on all the hard things that you've walked through, you have to remember all that God *has* done and focus on the good things. Going to bed thanking Him for what you *do* have and waking up thanking Him for everything all over again."

She went on to say that until we give up control, we'll be living with clenched hands, thinking we deserve better. And despite all our attempts to be faithful and obedient to God, maintaining an unrelenting grip on our own lives leaves no room for Jesus and the abundance of joy that He came to give us.

I was struck by my grandma's insight that trust and thankfulness go together. I was learning to be thankful, but giving up control and trusting God with my life was another story. I still struggle at times with looking beyond the frustration or pain. Seeing clearly through the storm is not something I do well. When we are faced with hardships, like losing a child or a terminal illness, it's not easy to acknowledge that God is in control. In fact, it's actually really hard. While God calls us to "live by faith, not by sight" (2 Cor. 5:7 NIV), it can feel as though we'll never learn how to adopt a mindset of inherent and automatic trust in Him.

I was struck by my grandma's insight that trust and thankfulness go together.

Going forward, this idea of merging trust and thankfulness really cut to the core of my frustrations. I started to realize that just because I've experienced trauma, I don't always have to hold my breath, waiting for the other shoe to drop. I can turn my clenched fists into open palms before the Lord and give Him control.

However, while it would be nice if we could just tell ourselves that God is in control and instantly change our entire mindset, that's not realistic. It's a daily choice coupled with some practical steps that we'll dive into later in the chapter. That realization led me to ask, "How do I know if my life is going to get any better?"

That might sound selfish, but I was on a hamster wheel of depression, thinking every year was going to get even harder. It was almost as if I had PTSD, causing me to be anxious about the future. So many bad things had happened in the past that I was questioning God and just waiting for the next awful thing to come my way. I thought life *was* about just suffering more and more for Jesus each year.

How could I release control and trust someone who had allowed this much pain? It was a very dark place that robbed me of all my joy.

But if my grandma could continue in joy after all she'd walked through, so could I. And I was determined to figure out how to joyfully relinquish control.

Balancing Trust and Personal Responsibility

Despite my determination, I found it hard to balance releasing control to the Lord with taking personal responsibility for my life. I have a driven, go-getter personality, so I constantly ask God, "What can I do? How can I fix this? What's next?" I think this is a valuable trait because we really do have more influence over our own lives than we sometimes think. God gave us brains, and I believe there are times when we are expected to make decisions and take action. We can't just sit around and expect God to give us explicit direction for every aspect of our lives. We can easily lose our spiritual drive if we mistake God's call to "quietness and trust" (Isa. 30:15 NIV) as permission to be passive. In other words, bench sitters. We might say, "Jesus, take the wheel," while doing nothing to advance His kingdom or our situation.

I have experienced seasons like that, when my inaction only made my circumstances harder. You may have heard the expression "Faith is not a spectator sport." We can't just clap for the players on the field when they score or sit back and take the punches that life throws at us. We can't complain but ultimately go with the flow, saying, "Well, it is what it is." If we do that, we'll be left asking, "What is the point in all this? Why even try?" And just like that, our joy is lost. So I lean toward actively trying to fix or improve my own situation.

However, because our God is sovereign, it is critical that we have a healthy balance between taking ownership and taking control. "We can make our plans, but the LORD determines our steps" (Proverbs 16:9). Man, that can be so hard to accept. I sometimes think that if I do my very best at controlling a situation, then maybe, just maybe, it won't end badly. I think that if I hold a life plan tightly or analyze all the ways to fix something, I might not have to experience pain all over again. I plan the best I can, prepare the best I can, do the best I can, and honestly become exhausted because of it. The problem is, we live in a broken world where evil, sin, and death still hold sway.

Despite doing everything "right" in my pregnancy, I still had a miscarriage.

You can eat healthy all the time but still get cancer.

You can be a "good Christian girl" but still be sexually abused.

Clearly, I understand that things don't always happen the way I want them to. But sometimes I find myself trapped in this line of thinking where I believe my life is so rough and always will be that I'm unable to see the things God *is* doing. That's why my grandma's reminder was so powerful for me. When I make a habit of thanking God for all He's done and is doing instead of dwelling on the pain, it demonstrates my faith and trust that He's worthy and in control.

Why was I living as if I had no choice or power to change my own circumstances? I think I was exhausted from trying again and again to trust that my joy would be restored. Even today, I still try to find the balance between giving God control and controlling everything myself. Through that process of "trying so hard," I put a burden on my back that is not mine to carry. In Proverbs, we are instructed to "trust in the LORD with all your heart and lean not on your own understanding; in all your ways submit to him, and he will make your paths straight" (3:5–6 NIV). Our lives won't be pain-free, but we will be guided by our heavenly Father along the path He has laid out for us.

When we release control and let God work, we'll be surprised by how much happier we are as joy remains the constant.

Learning Trust

In marriage, trusting the Lord and giving up control take on a whole new meaning. When I met Andrew, he was slowly transitioning out of the navy to pursue a medical degree. At the time, I thought how wonderful it would be to marry a doctor with a military background. I imagined the level of peace and security it would bring.

So many things sound perfect at first: buying a dog, starting a new job, moving to a new house, taking on a new role, or going on a vacation. But sometimes when reality plays out, we're left thinking, *How in the world did I get here? This is the worst.* We start with big dreams and good intentions. But after the initial excitement wears off, we can face financial, emotional, mental, or even spiritual obstacles.

What I thought was going to bring me so much joy and happiness brought a lot of challenges. When Andrew started medical school, we were on a pretty tight budget and already had a one-year-old child. We knew we wanted more kids but didn't want to wait another seven years until he completed his training, so we decided to keep growing our family. By the middle of his third year of medical school, we had grown to a family of five.

However, because of his schedule, we hardly saw him. I was practically raising our kids by myself. To make matters worse, we moved twice during the first couple years of medical school. There was no consistency in our lives. Schedules and routines were constantly changing, and I had a hard time investing myself in anything where I was. I rarely slept when my husband worked the night shift, and I struggled with anxiety and depression. I truly thought this season would never end. My heart wasn't in a thankful or trusting place. If only I had known that my soul would feel lighter if my hands were unclenched.

Over time, my joy was restored as I learned to let go. While I would have liked it to be an overnight change, I had to make a daily choice to allow God to truly take over. Below are some of the steps I take that help me live a life of joy even when everything around me seems out of control.

1. Let Go of the Outcome

Accept that suffering will come, but always cling to the fact that Jesus is close and is walking with us. Yes, it will be difficult. Yes, there will be suffering. Yes, we will do everything we can to make it perfect ... but life happens and it will be rough at times. I can't tell you how many times we've put together a one- or two-year plan only to have life turn out completely different than we thought. We can be wise and plan and schedule, but remember to leave room for God to work. Let's schedule in space for more of God's surprises and less of our structured life.

2. Look at Life with Eternal Eyes

In the big scheme of things, all the little details that we stress over don't really matter compared to eternity. If we remember why we're here on earth—to glorify God and make disciples—we'll be more inclined to trust Him.

3. Humble Yourself

This is a hard step to take because until we realize that His plans are better than ours, we'll skip right over it. When we humble ourselves, we open our palms and say, "Let Your will be done, Lord," regardless of our present circumstances.

4. Do Only What You Can

Sometimes life hits hard with struggles, and we can't imagine there is joy to be had in such rough circumstances. In those cases, we can only take it one day at a time ... one moment at a time sometimes ... making the daily choice to trust God. I'm not going to pretend I do this perfectly or even very

well. I have learned that some burdens I was carrying for years weren't mine to bear. But we can only
work on these steps the best we can and let God
do the rest. When we let God work, we'll see His
strength and mighty hand at work in our lives.

But getting here, to this better outlook on trust and releasing
control, took a lot of effort. I cried a lot of tears, wrestled through a
lot of trials, and had many difficult conversations with my husband
and the Lord. I wrote a list of the things our family could look forward to after my husband finished his medical training and landed
a permanent position. It was important for me to take some time to
dream a little, to look past our current reality. I also needed a healthy
dose of discernment so that I knew who to listen to and talk to so
that I didn't feel so alone. While I felt isolated at times because of my
husband's schedule, there were actually more women than I realized
who were walking through something similar.

To discover inner peace and joy, I had to stand in confidence,
knowing God has a beautiful story for me despite what I was feeling
in the moment. I had to accept my circumstances and not wish them
away while simultaneously taking responsibility, looking outside
myself, and modeling stability for my children. And even though
I've had years of waking up in the middle of the night alone, sweating and scared, because of my past trauma, I know God is with me
and this won't last forever. This too shall pass.

I love the reminder in 2 Corinthians 4:17–18: "Our light and
momentary troubles are achieving for us an eternal glory that far

outweighs them all. So we fix our eyes not on what is seen, but on what is unseen, since what is seen is temporary, but what is unseen is eternal" (NIV).

> ## We can be wise and plan and schedule, but remember to leave room for God to work.

We have choices, and we can learn to pray for more courage and determination and gumption so we're fighting women, not fragile women who break when hard things come our way. I want to be a woman who is hopeful about the future while appreciating the season I'm in. Trusting God and releasing control are great first steps to becoming a fighter.

The Role of Choice

While circumstances are often out of our control, we serve a God who gave us free will. Therefore, we have a *choice* about how we'll respond to virtually everything. He isn't forcing us to do or say anything. He is no puppet master, dictating every aspect of our lives.

When it comes to making wise decisions about everything from our health, to being good stewards of our time, to acting respectably and responsibly in this world, to parenting our kids, we can pray that God would lead us in each of these areas, but He won't force Himself in. He is waiting for us to ask for His guidance.

Picture this: You worked for years on a beautiful design for a home. You designed it all by yourself because, well, you know best! You developed the perfect layout and color scheme and planned to use the finest materials. You spent all your free time dreaming of and designing this home—your forever home. Every room was thoroughly, beautifully, and meticulously planned to the best of your ability. At least, that's what you thought.

One day, your hard work paid off and your dream came true. After saving enough money, you actually started to build it all by yourself! Despite countless days of backbreaking manual labor, you managed to lay the foundation, frame out the structure and install the roof, complete the plumbing and electrical, and hang the drywall. Your home is looking amazing and is almost 75 percent complete.

At the last minute, you decide to get a contractor involved, just to make sure you haven't forgotten a tiny detail or two. The contractor looks over your entire home, taking lots of measurements and making lots of notes. After inspecting every nook and cranny from the attic to the crawl space, he sits you down with a concerned look on his face.

He describes how the electrical work doesn't meet code. The windows aren't sealed properly and will likely leak when it rains. The plumbing is already showing signs of corrosion. The foundation is faulty and already cracking. Worst of all, the contractor is concerned that you won't even get the chance to enjoy your new home before it crumbles to the ground, burns down, or blows away in a storm.

What would you do? Would you thank the contractor for all the warnings and fix the issues? Or would you say, "Forget it—it's fine as is. I'm just going to go ahead and finish it." After all, you know best, right?

In a similar way, we treat Jesus as our last-minute contractor. Sometimes, as Christians, we act as if His instructions and corrections are mere suggestions and as if we know best. Even worse, we make decisions our entire lives and then blame God for our mistakes and lack of trust. Instead of leaving room for Him to work, we act out of arrogance and mistrust, thinking our lives are better when we're in charge.

Our lives are always better with Jesus; our lives are never better when we're in control.

He is not going to take a sledgehammer to your perfectly ship-lapped wall. No. He wants you to have the most beautiful house, but if you already built it without Him, it's going to be even harder to tear down and start fresh. When we're sitting in the middle of a broken, messed-up house, we have to trust that God is going to restore it.

Depending on our personality types, releasing that type of control can be excruciating and a blow to our pride. But here's the deal: God doesn't want us sitting on the ground, crying because our houses are collapsing around us. He wants us to get up and help Him rebuild. He grabs our hands, gives us some gloves and tools, and says, "Let's do this together."

We don't get to see the blueprint that God envisions and tailors for each of us. But in the end, it's going to be exactly what we *need*, with unexpected features that we never would have chosen, such as a skylight in our office or a window in the kitchen so we can see the sunrise perfectly while we make our coffee every morning. While the house might be smaller and simpler than we planned, He already thought about all the details we had missed or never could have envisioned.

And another thing—God won't let anything go to waste. His plan is so much better than ours that releasing the job to Him will be freeing and the best decision we can make. It's going to take submission, obedience, patience, and trust that God knows exactly what He's doing.

God promises good things for us. Our lives are going to be beautiful, even if they look different than we expected. "We are God's masterpiece. He has created us anew in Christ Jesus, so we can do the good things he planned for us long ago" (Eph. 2:10). As much as we hate to admit it, we don't know what's best for our own lives. "Jesus deserves far more glory than Moses, just as a person who builds a house deserves more praise than the house itself. For every house has a builder, but the one who built everything is God" (Heb. 3:3–4).

God wants to build our homes on His solid foundation. It'll take work. Don't forget the choices we'll have to make throughout the process and that building a house with the Lord is a lifelong venture. There will always be things to work on. It will never be perfect, but growth happens in the process. When we give up control, we'll learn to enjoy the process and relish the fact that Jesus is close and always willing to extend a helping hand. Thankfully, God's Spirit is also ushering us into what's best if we are diligent in asking for His guidance.

When our lives seem out of control, we can find comfort in trusting the God who understands. Our understanding of life and how things should work is so limited compared to God's. He's a God of miracles, who has always existed and will always be seated on His throne. He created this world and gives breath to our lungs. Placing our trust in Him is not only the humble thing to do but also what we are called to do.

But I get it. When you've lost trust in people and the world, it's hard to trust God. When hard things come our way, it's extremely difficult to get back in the game with the same trust and determination we had before.

But that is life. *Full* of the hard and messy. *Full* of both pain and joy. It's difficult to accept that while we have breath, we'll face hardships. In his epistle, James wrote, "Consider it pure joy, my brothers and sisters, whenever you face trials of many kinds, because you know that the testing of your faith produces perseverance" (1:2–3 NIV). In this life, we will be confronted by things we never wanted.

Nothing is a surprise to God. Nothing shocks Him. There is nothing He can't handle. Nothing is too small for Him to care about. No situation is too far gone.

We can't handle what life throws at us on our own. We may be given more than we can handle just so we experience His comfort and love unlike any other time. God is gracious and we can trust His plan to restore us. We can't save ourselves. We can't trust our own plans. But when we release control and ask Him, God will comfort us, help us, and direct us in the way we should go. Psalm 94:19 says, "When anxiety was great within me, your consolation brought me joy" (NIV). Entrusting our burdens, anger, questions, and sadness to Him will restore our joy. We can choose to live with unclenched hands regardless of what comes our way, allowing Him to work in our lives.

I think of how many times I've told my children, "If you had just listened to me! Mama knows best." How I wish they could get it into their heads that the boundaries I set are for their benefit and out of love. In spite of my love for them, I have to let go of the ultimate outcome because they have the freedom to make their own choices. God loves me infinitely more than I can love my own kids, yet He won't dictate what I should do even though He knows best. Although I still struggle at times with relinquishing control, I can be reminded to sit with my grandma in my parents' backyard and think, *What a beautiful life.*

I pray that, despite the sadness and pain in our lives, we can focus on all the good God has done, knowing our lives are in His hands. I pray that we can thank Him for all the blessings and remember His plans will always be better than ours. Our problems and pain will never disappear in this life, but living with open hands will bring us joy in the long run.

reflections

Take Action

Where in your life do you need to relinquish control? If you try to structure everything, you are taking on a heavy burden that is not yours to bear. Today, take a step back, and if needed, schedule in space for more of God's surprises.

Key Verse

"Our light and momentary troubles are achieving for us an eternal glory that far outweighs them all. So we fix our eyes not on what is seen, but on what is unseen, since what is seen is temporary, but what is unseen is eternal." (2 Cor. 4:17–18 NIV)

Closing Prayer

Lord, I so desperately want my life to go well. I want to be healthy and live comfortably. I want my family to be taken care of and enjoy their lives. But my good intentions often lead me to take on more than I can possibly handle. I confess that I don't leave enough room for Your Spirit to work. Help me to always be humble and discerning, confident that You are in control. I know You are here for me. No amount of my own work will save me. Regardless of what happens in the future, I pray that Your Spirit will guide and lead me. Give me wisdom. Help me to relinquish control and trust You, embracing the freedom and joy that come when I commit everything to You.

avoid comparison

Bracelets and Stickers

In retrospect, the hemorrhoid was what did me in. How could such a small thing on my body make me feel so bad about myself? Well, let me complete the picture for you: I hadn't had time to shower, my hair was greasy, I was dealing with a random zit from eating one too many chocolate chip cookies, and I kept forgetting to pluck a black hair on my chin.

I was wearing my husband's oversized sweatshirt with leggings. It was comfortable, had a zipper that provided easy access for nursing, and made me feel close to him since we hadn't seen him in a few days due to his work schedule. I had thrown on a hat to cover my hair.

Some mothers call this their "mom uniform," except I didn't feel like I was pulling it off. I wanted to call it my "slob outfit." My "lazy outfit." My "don't-judge-me outfit." Or even my "I'm-fine-don't-ask outfit." Clearly, I didn't feel good about myself.

While our thoughts of comparison can come from anywhere, including our mommy groups, our workplaces, or even our churches, I find that in the age of the smartphone they increasingly come from social media. That is exactly where I found myself that morning, which was one of the worst things I could have done. Now what did I see? Flawless faces with freshly highlighted (and washed) hair, perfect smiles featuring straight pearly whites. Photos of kids in matching outfits with everyone (even the family dog) looking at the camera. Someone's spotless, squeaky-clean home and the most beautiful panoramic vacation photos. To top it all off, these women appeared to have not only perfect lives but also incredibly successful businesses!

Clearly, I couldn't keep up with the world's demands. Why was I scrolling through my newsfeed when I knew it would only make me feel worse?

We all know social media is basically a highlight reel, and we're all guilty of posting our best instead of reality. Most of us will be attracted to pretty things, like matching outfits and pleasing color schemes. But we also know every woman goes through rough patches on both a large and a small scale: the breakup, the diagnosis, the dirty house, the exhaustion … at the end of the day, we're comparing ourselves based on those perfect photos. We're contrasting our worst day with another person's best.

We're not drawn to the messiness, because it's what we see every day. Most people don't want to see the gunk behind your kitchen sink or the chunky baby spit-up all over your shirt. We're looking for a break from reality, not more of it.

What we *do* want to gain from social media is the feeling that we're not alone. We all have an innate desire to be known, valued, and respected. We also want to feel seen and understood in our roles or our suffering. While these desires are not inherently sinful, we can quickly get off course when we seek external validation instead of going to God. Social media (i.e., the world) will never fill that void and our longing to be known. We can become so caught up in seeking this validation that we get things backward.

Instead, we must decrease for Him in order to increase in our lives (see John 3:30 ESV). And it's in that process of humility that we find our true worth, rather than in comparing our lives to others'. As Paul wrote in Philippians, "This same God ... will supply all your needs from his glorious riches, which have been given to us in Christ Jesus" (4:19).

Social media causes us to forget what's right in front of us: our daily bread. We forget about God, but He was not meant to be placed on the back burner. The Lord has set us apart for a specific purpose. Yet I've found that when I'm distracted looking at everyone else's posts, I end up getting jealous, not to mention wasting precious time.

What is the result of this cycle? The comparison game, which robs us of our joy.

Contentment versus Comparison

If you know me, you know I'm a great start-up girl. I'm down to help you start anything. You have an idea? I'll help you make it a reality. You want to start a business? I'll help you find a way. But when it comes to seeing things through to the very end, I'm prone to lose focus. The ins and outs and details bog me down. Whereas others have the endurance to build a business or continue other endeavors for the long-term, I prefer to switch things up and move on to the next project.

Over the last several years, success followed me in some areas, but I never felt important or seen. Although I used social media to promote these various endeavors, I began to fall into comparison. I saw so many amazing women thriving in their niches. I found it easy to mistake their growing influence for shining brightly for Jesus (see Matthew 5:16). If they were finding success but I wasn't, it must mean I wasn't as aligned with Christ as they were. But my problem was that I interpreted their examples as a directive to "go and do all the things, Nicole. Be known."

As you can imagine, that exhausted me and robbed me of joy. As Christians, of course we are to represent Christ *in* all things, but that doesn't mean we need to *do* all things. And it most definitely doesn't mean that we should be praised and known in a way that takes the focus off God and puts it on ourselves. When I dug down to the root of my discontent, I didn't necessarily want what these women had, but I did want the *feeling* of accomplishment that surely comes with achievement. In a very selfish, nonholy way, I wanted to feel known and finally see the fruits of my labor—and it was stealing my joy.

I sometimes feel like I do so much and don't see any rewards for all that I'm doing. Do you ever feel like that? At times, I'm so spent at the end of the day that all I do is look back and think, *Am I even making a difference? Will all this work for my kids (for my boss, for my parents, etc.) ever pay off?* These questions have driven me to look for a job outside the home in some seasons. Receiving a paycheck and thriving in the business world seemed very desirable. I wanted to feel accomplished and noticed. I wanted to dress up in professional attire and swipe a badge to get into my office. I wanted to lead important meetings and be considered essential.

Without little rewards, daily accomplishments, or glimpses of progress along the way, I was prone to give up. I compared myself with other women and even other moms. Women who are amazing moms *and work* a full-time job. Moms *who also run* a successful business. Moms *who were also* starting impactful ministries.

While I love the idea of being a successful woman, why did I think I had to be a mom *and* something else? It was important for me to be content with my God-given role as a mother, but I wasn't content because I didn't feel seen. And when we don't feel seen or content, we often look other places for validation.

As with so many other struggles ... healing and recovery started with a thankful heart.

I wish I could tell you there is a secret to avoiding comparison. The truth is, I finally stopped the comparison and found contentment after I remembered all that I have been given. As with so many other struggles in my life with the Lord, healing and recovery started with a thankful heart. God had given me so much and was doing so much in my life, yet I was too busy looking around at everyone else to notice what was right in front of me.

So I finally became the girl who cherished what was right in front of her. First, I identified what was most important to me: being a wife and mother. Second, I tried to actively focus on thriving in these God-given roles before tackling other things. Some days I didn't accomplish anything except being a present mom. Some days I rested, and other days I checked off all my to-dos and made the best meals for my family. But I think that *is* the secret to avoiding comparison: being content with what's right in front of us with a joyful heart.

While contentment sounds simple, I realize it's incredibly difficult, and I still often struggle with it. However, it's all about our heart motives, not our accomplishments. Our calling and purpose are right before us. Being faithful with what we have is the key to feeling content, instead of comparing. Being faithful in your job. Being faithful in motherhood. Being faithful in your schooling. Being faithful in marriage. Whatever your role is right now, be faithful in it and do the best you can.

A Secure Identity

How do we become secure in who we are in Christ while cheering other people on? How do we *really* do this?

Most importantly, we need to know our identity in Christ. "You are a chosen people. You are royal priests, a holy nation, God's very own possession. As a result, you can show others the goodness of God, for he called you out of the darkness into his wonderful light" (1 Pet. 2:9). When our confidence comes from Him and Him only, our goal becomes glorifying God rather than pleasing people. We recognize that we are set apart, messy but holy, and that we are each made uniquely. It's a growing confidence in Him. When we walk in our giftings and who He made us to be (regardless of our perceived value from the world's perspective), we can be secure. In Christ, we are enough and wanted.

God wired each one of us differently, which means there is no carbon copy of you out there. That should bring you joy! Every fingerprint is unique and every life matters to God. While God has everything He needs, He *wanted* to include us in His plan of redemption for the world. All Christians are a part of the body of Christ, with each of us bringing our own set of strengths and weaknesses to the table.

When Jesus called the disciples, He put together twelve seemingly random men who had many different abilities and backgrounds. There were a tax collector, a few fishermen, a doubter, an over-thinker, a fighter, an oddball, and more. God brought together men who were on different journeys to follow Jesus. Imagine if God had gathered twelve brothers from the same family, from the same city, with the same upbringing and occupation. Yes, their personalities would have probably still been different, but there would have been such competition and less diversity of gifts to draw from!

I believe that's why Jesus chose twelve ordinary but very different people to be His disciples. I believe He wanted to show that we all have something unique to offer when we submit to Christ. When we know whose we are and who we are serving, our mission to glorify God and make disciples becomes clear no matter who's watching, applauding, or listening. All that approval stuff is dust in the wind.

Ultimately, our identity in Christ comes down to the inner confidence that we have in the Lord—secure in who God made us to be. Not who we think we are or want to be (because that can change daily), but aligned with how God *made* us, at our core. Chosen, set apart, and His. That's why the second we use social media to fill our confidence bucket, we'll be left feeling emptier than when we started. The world tells you to go places other than the feet of Jesus for validation. The focus shifts from God to ourselves. When we recognize that we are undeserving and remain humble, we remain secure at the feet of Jesus. If we're regularly running after the right thing, it becomes easier to discern when we're chasing the approval of the world.

The world tells you to go places other than the feet of Jesus for validation.

Another reason social media will rob us of joy is that it gives plenty of skewed perspectives, half-truths, and incomplete information. Have you ever come away from time spent scrolling thinking any of these things?

I am dead in my sins.
I am not enough.
I am a wretched human.
I have nothing to offer God; He doesn't need me.

For someone who doesn't know the full truth of our life with Christ, statements like these can seem depressing. They can cause you to seek value elsewhere. We can't let these lies distract us from who we are in Him, because that is worth celebrating and being joyful about. Let's change these sentences above to reflect the full truth:

> While we were dead in our sins, we are now *alive* in Christ! (see Rom. 6:11)
>
> While we aren't enough on our own, God's grace is sufficient for us. (see 2 Cor. 12:9 NIV)
>
> While we are wretched humans without God, Jesus paid it all and now we can be seen as blameless before the Father because of His sacrifice. (see John 3:16–17; Phil. 2:14–16 NIV)
>
> While we have nothing to offer God, He wanted us and loves us more than we'll ever know! (see Ps. 52:8)

Let's stay balanced and live in confidence, knowing and proclaiming the full truth. We can walk in freedom and victory, humility and joy because of what Christ has done. We can enjoy each blessing and cling to Him when hard things come our way. We can come as weak and needy humans before the Lord but leave restored and full of the Spirit. We have Christ in us, the hope of glory (see Col. 1:27), and that means we are worth far more than rubies (see Prov. 31:10) and are more valuable than the sparrows (see

Matt. 6:26). We are made in God's image (see Gen. 1:27) and called by Christ to make disciples (see Matt. 28:19).

We will find purpose and fulfillment as we partner with Christ to live for Him. I've never been more joyful than when I walk with the confidence of Christ while also acknowledging my depravity.

Focus on What's in Front of You

I can think of multiple examples in the Bible of women who had a difficult time with comparison. For starters, Sarah didn't think she would ever have babies, so she gave her maidservant, Hagar, to her husband, Abraham. Then when Hagar became pregnant, which was the point, Sarah mistreated her and complained to Abraham. When God told Abraham He was going to give Sarah a son, she laughed and doubted the power of God (see Gen. 16–18).

We can learn from Sarah that when we go outside the Lord's purpose and will for our lives, we cause problems for ourselves. Not only is aligning ourselves with Christ the safest place to land, but it also will bring us the most peace and joy.

You may also know the story of Leah, the plain older sister, and Rachel, who had "a beautiful figure and a lovely face" (Gen. 29:17). But they were competing for the same man! When their father tricked Jacob into marrying Leah first, even though it was Rachel he wanted, Leah became jealous of Jacob's love for Rachel. Yet Leah was the fertile one who was having all the babies. Rachel was barren and became jealous of Leah, wishing God would give her a son. "When Rachel saw that she was not bearing Jacob any children, she became jealous of her sister. So she said to Jacob, 'Give me children, or I'll die!'" (30:1 NIV).

That doesn't sound like she was in a joyful and contented state of mind but instead was depressed, sad, and thinking only of what she lacked. Both women wanted love, attention, and children. Sound familiar? We all want to be loved, valued, and noticed. But sometimes life doesn't go the way we want, and we become discontent because our own plans for our lives are thwarted. Comparison makes us doubt God as we question "Is He really enough?" Then the Enemy tempts us into thinking we need more. The lies pour in as we begin thinking what more we "need" and how good we'll feel if we just have …

- a little more money
- a better job
- a healthier body
- a bigger house
- a prettier backyard
- a flawless face
- one more kid
- a bigger social media platform

Those things are fine if we feel led to work toward them, but when they become our primary focus, we can get caught in the comparison trap instead of focusing on what God has in front of us.

Every person you see on social media has his or her own journey with the Lord, and yours is just as unique and exciting. Let's stop investing our emotions in people we don't really know. Let's start investing in lives that reflect God's unique purpose for us. We want the life God has for us.

I know you moms are probably thinking, *Nicole, I'm surrounded by children all day, I haven't showered in days, and I don't even know the last time I talked to an adult.* I get it. But your work is seen by the Lord. So instead of going on social media to look at all the things you label a "big deal," what if you started looking at your children and saying, "Wow, now *this* job is a BIG DEAL!" Or what if you showed up to your job, where you feel unappreciated and depleted, with the confidence that God has placed you there in this season to be faithful and obedient? Let's carry the confidence of Christ, knowing that we're in this season for a reason and that God will use us in bigger ways than we can imagine.

We may not all be moms here, but this idea still applies across the board. We need to understand that the size of our ministries, social media followings, bank accounts, friends lists, and so on doesn't matter. If you're obedient and faithful to what God has put in front of you, that's all that matters. The world wants us to play the numbers-and-likes game, but having an eternal perspective means emphasizing obedience and faithfulness.

We can't celebrate each other until we are content with where we are. Personally, it took me awhile to get there, but when I finally landed, I was a better wife, mom, writer, and friend because I was walking on the path God led me on and my joy was restored.

Remember my missions trip to Nepal when I was in college? Well, some young girls I met at a children's home there drastically changed my perspective on finding contentment. I returned to America determined to keep my focus on the important things of life.

On the last day of the trip, several girls grabbed my hands and led me up to their room, where they gave me gifts. I sat down on the cool cement floor as each new friend of mine walked over to her drawer, pulled out something special for me from a tin can, and gave me a treasure to remember her by.

"Here, sister Nicole!"

With excitement in their eyes and joy in their smiles, they gave me bracelets and stickers and barrettes and the cutest homemade notes. They had very little, yet they gave me everything. I had so much and felt like I gave them nothing.

The humility and love I felt from their acts of kindness and joyful giving was astonishing. Here I was, a college girl with my own car, bedroom, and closet full of clothes, and yet their generous gestures showed me how easily my eyes drift from Jesus.

These girls reminded me of the poor widow in Mark 12:41–44, who put two small coins into the temple treasury. While it was a small amount compared to the donations of others, she brought all she had because she knew it was worth giving the King of Kings everything she possessed. I want to be like that. Instead of comparing myself with those around me, I just want to offer my King everything I have.

I want to be content in all circumstances so that my life is open for the Lord to lead me. Think of the ways God will use us when we're satisfied in Him! Paul wrote in the book of Philippians:

> I am not saying this because I am in need, for I have learned to be content whatever the circumstances. I know what it is to be in need, and I know what it is to have plenty. I have learned the secret of being content in any and every situation, whether

well fed or hungry, whether living in plenty or in
want. (4:11–12 NIV)

Not only does the Lord see the little things, but He rejoices to
see the work begin. Instead of comparing our bad days to everyone else's best days, let's remember that our lives are a journey with
the Lord as He leads us to our best. It might not be popular or go
viral. You might not be a CEO or a mom of three as you hoped.
You might not land the dream job or succeed in your start-up. But
God has you. Let's strive for holiness, not visibility. "Do not despise
these small beginnings, for the LORD rejoices to see the work begin"
(Zech. 4:10).

> **Instead of comparing our bad
> days to everyone else's best
> days, let's remember our lives
> are a journey with the Lord
> as He leads us to our best.**

We can become women who thrive regardless of our circumstances. We're all on the same playing field regardless of what the
world is telling us. Regardless of the number of friends we have,
how we decorate our homes, the size of our social media followings,
the behavior of our children, or the growth of our ministries, we're
all made in the image of God. Let's stop taking ourselves out of the

game because we're not *feeling* valued. Rest secure in the knowledge that you *are* valued.

I pray that we walk in the confidence and contentment of Christ. I pray that we take small and faithful steps today as we walk in obedience to what's right in front of us. And most of all, I pray we remember that we are wanted and valued by a God who adores each one of us. When we believe that without a doubt, true joy will follow.

reflections

Take Action

Are you comparing yourself to someone else? If so, take a step back and evaluate whether you're content in the roles God has given you. Are you content with the life you have? Do you need to make some adjustments to your routine, responsibilities, or roles to experience more contentment? Remember, you are on your own individual journey with Jesus and it's as important as the journey of anyone else who seems to be further along.

Key Verse

"I am not saying this because I am in need, for I have learned to be content whatever the circumstances. I know what it is to be in need, and I know what it is to have plenty. I have learned the secret of being content in any and every situation, whether well fed or hungry, whether living in plenty or in want." (Phil. 4:11–12 NIV)

Closing Prayer

Lord, I confess my discontented heart to You today. You've given me a beautiful life, and I have so much to be thankful for. Yet I still become jealous of others sometimes. Create in me a new heart, and renew a steadfast spirit in me that is full of grace and contentment in You. Help me to remain secure in my identity while cheering others on. Build my confidence in You so that Your truth becomes my solid foundation. Help me to focus on the people and plans You've put in front of me. Thank You for all You're doing in my life.

the purpose in the pain

It was a blazing-hot, ninety-five-degree summer day in North Carolina. I was about twenty weeks pregnant, and our growing family of five decided we should go on a walk. My husband was home, a rarity at the time, and I thought it would be a fun outing.

Within five minutes, I was dripping with sweat, wondering why in the world we decided to do this.

My two oldest boys were on their bikes, and my youngest was on his scooter. If you're a mom, you probably know what happened next. The kids decided halfway through that they'd rather be walking, or at home, or at Disneyland. The whining and bad attitudes escalated dramatically.

"Mom, can you hold my sunglasses?"

"Dad, can you carry my scooter?"

"Mom, I want to go back home. I wish we could go to the pool."

Finally I'd had it. My husband and I were carrying all our kids' things, and as we turned the corner, my oldest started complaining.

"That way is all uphill. I don't want to go uphill!"

From behind me, my husband responded, "If we don't go uphill, you can never enjoy going fast downhill on the way back."

Despite my sweaty stomach and sore arms, I realized the profound truth in what my husband had just said.

My life had felt like one long uphill battle for the past decade.

But I didn't want my whole life to be an uphill climb anymore. I needed some breaks along the way, some downhill excitement, and some joy to keep me going.

Living a faithful Christian life is no piece of cake. It's so much easier to live for yourself and do whatever you want than to walk in obedience to the Lord. I thought it would be easier to shove my pain away, power through trials, and do things in my own strength.

The difficulties I endured changed everything. I was focused on my pain and my unknown future, and over the years, I'd become a very negative person who I didn't even recognize.

But now I see so clearly that the Enemy was elated when pain came my way.

When I was raped, the Enemy wanted me to stay in my darkness so that I'd never see myself as whole again.

When I was surrounded by broken relationships, the Enemy wanted me to believe that people can never change.

When I had a miscarriage, the Enemy wanted me to believe that God didn't have my best interests at heart.

When I was diagnosed with cancer and going through severe depression, the Enemy wanted me to end my life.

And so on.

The Bible tells us that the Devil comes to steal, kill, and destroy us (see John 10:10), and he will never stop. With every trial I have faced, the Enemy has been smiling, hoping this would be the thing that makes me turn from Christ.

But what do I see when I look back? I see that God has been with me through every trial. By His grace, He worked miracles in my heart and restored my joy despite the pain. He gave me a purpose when I felt like my life was meaningless, and He will do the same for you.

In our most challenging moments, it's easy to forget the joy, freedom, and victory of a life with Christ. But I can look back now and celebrate all that He's given me. I can see how He surprised me with a better plan and healed me from past trauma. I can see how God has restored my life and renewed my joy. None of this would have happened without a relationship with Him.

Wisdom is cultivated.
Endurance is learned.

When we respond to Jesus with obedience, we will discover the purpose in our pain. When we remind ourselves to study the Word, know God's character, forgive quickly, serve others, see the bigger picture, take time to rest and heal, take personal responsibility, stop complaining, give up control, and avoid comparison, I believe we will be well on our way to experiencing God-given joy despite our trials. If we take a step back, we can see what God is doing in and through us and how He has worked on our behalf regardless of dire situations. We see how our pain makes us stronger. And most importantly, we see how even the worst things make us more like Christ.

My unique story has equipped me to understand women who have been sexually abused. I have experienced reconciliation with my dad and have been taught through difficulties the power of forgiveness and letting go. I relate to so many cancer survivors. I can hold a friend and truly feel her pain when she's lost a child through miscarriage. I can be someone's voice when she feels emotionally abused by those once closest to her. I have grown from these experiences and seen God's justice firsthand. If none of these hard things had happened to me, I wouldn't be able to see God's goodness and have the confidence to help others better know the truth of the gospel and point them to Christ.

Wisdom is cultivated. Endurance is learned. The suffering we face and the way we navigate it reveals our spiritual maturity. As the Bible says, "When troubles of any kind come your way, consider it an opportunity for great joy. For you know that when your faith is tested, your endurance has a chance to grow. So let it grow" (James 1:2–4).

Hard things have the power to bring us closer to the Lord … if we'll let them. Our natural inclination is to avoid difficulties at all costs, but knowing hardships *will* happen, we can normalize the suffering and have joy in all seasons. Trials will come, and we can either make the Enemy smile as we lose our faith or continue walking with the Lord until we hear Him say, "Well done, good and faithful servant," at the end of our lives. That is all I want.

The best part is that God chooses to *use* us in our weaknesses, shortcomings, sickness, and depression. He provides opportunities for us to learn and grow. He lavishes His blessings on us in ways we could have never imagined. He chooses to love us even though we are undeserving. God in His loving-kindness still involves us in His great and beautiful plan—if we are willing.

God with Us

I find the story of Moses extremely reassuring. Despite Moses's doubts and fears, God remained gracious and involved in his life. Moses doubted God (see Ex. 3:11), questioned His plan (4:1), thought he was unqualified (v. 10), and even ended a conversation with God by saying, "Pardon your servant, Lord. Please send someone else" (v. 13 NIV). Yet God *still* used him. Can you believe that?

Over and over again, God involved Moses and Aaron in miracles and in His grand plan to free the Israelites from slavery in Egypt.

"The LORD said to him, 'What is that in your hand?' 'A staff,' he replied. The LORD said, 'Throw it on the ground.' Moses threw it on the ground and it became a snake, and he ran from it" (vv. 2–3 NIV).

God instructed Moses to use what he already had—what was literally *in his hand*—to demonstrate God's power and liberate His people. Moses's clean hand became diseased (v. 6), and his staff turned into a snake (v. 4). Aaron summoned frogs by stretching out his staff (8:5–6), and the plague of gnats came when he struck the dusty ground (vv. 16–17).

While God is powerful enough to do anything on His own, His desire is ultimately to *use* His people to make His glory known throughout the world and in the lives right before us.

That is what our lives are all about. Making Christ known. Even in our suffering, even in our tears, even in our pain, even in our questions. Because there may be no reason for our pain except "that the works of God might be displayed" (John 9:3 NIV).

That is what our lives are all about. Making Christ known. Even in our suffering.

And we have to be okay with that. I personally will never get to a place where I'm "okay" with pain, but it's about being made more like Christ. It's about His glory, not ours. His crown, not our own. His words of truth, not "my truth." His power revealed, not our personal agenda. Following Jesus means dying to ourselves, surrendering our desires, and being made completely new.

That is where true joy is found. While the world preaches self-love and lies, Jesus is whispering "Come." The joy that awaits us is a newfound understanding and a new way of life (see 2 Cor. 5:17).

As C. S. Lewis wrote in *Mere Christianity*,

> The Christian way is different: harder, and easier.
> Christ says, "Give me All. I don't want so much
> of your time and so much of your money and so
> much of your work: I want You. I have not come
> to torment your natural self, but to kill it. No half-
> measures are any good. I don't want to cut off a
> branch here and a branch there, I want to have the
> whole tree down…. Hand over the whole natural

self, all the desires which you think innocent as well as the ones you think wicked—the whole outfit. I will give you a new self instead. In fact, I will give you Myself: my own will shall become yours."[1]

This is the theme I've seen echoed throughout the entire Bible and my own life: God is with us in our suffering, fighting for us. He is not just with us, but He hears us, He sees us, He has not forgotten us, and He has a plan. Best of all, if we surrender to Him, our dark lives will become beaming lights for Christ. Beaming!

That all sounds great, I know. But life can seem way too heavy at times, and the last thing we want to hear is the truth. When those times come, because they will, I invite you to walk in obedience, remember the truth of God's words, and sit at the feet of Christ, even if you're angry. But don't stay there. Although you can always come before the Lord as you are, you need to get up and work out your salvation in spite of your doubts. C. S. Lewis tells us that "we have to be continually reminded of what we believe. Neither this belief nor any other will automatically remain alive in the mind. It must be fed."[2]

We ourselves are not strong enough to get through our trials alone. We need to work out our salvation because God is serious about holiness and obedience. In all things, even when it's rough. We don't get a pass because we're going through something hard. It's actually in that spot of wanting to give up that we grow spiritually.

I never want to second-guess God's purpose for my life. And I never want to miss out on His healing.

Just because life is difficult doesn't mean we should sit back as though we were purposeless with a distant God. It doesn't mean we should just grin and bear it either. We have a calling to permeate the culture with Jesus, actively fighting evil as citizens of heaven.[3] Focusing on this higher purpose will help us get out of our ruts. Seeing the purpose in our pain and walking in obedience go hand in hand.

Sometimes we need to forgive, or stop complaining, or sit awhile with Jesus. Sometimes we need to remember what God has done or see the beauty around us. But then we need to keep going. Exodus 14:15 says, "The LORD said to Moses, 'Why are you crying out to me? Tell the Israelites to move on'" (NIV). While the Israelites were complaining and panicking about how they'd be delivered from the Egyptians, God was like, "Hey, get moving!"

Maybe you need to hear that today, when the world is spinning fast and you're doubting your role or are mired in your struggles. How are we supposed to take what we've been given—all our pain, our past, our strengths and weaknesses, our family and friendships—and make it all beautiful? How do we smile through it all and have our joy restored? The answer is *we* don't.

God does.

Living in the Tension

I have become comfortable living in this space—between intimacy with Christ and being repelled by hardships. This spiritual tug of war of pulling closer to Christ, hands almost bleeding from the tight grip, but also wanting to let go and give up, no pain but no victory either.

If I've learned anything over the past decade, it's that I'm starting to crave the fight because of what it produces. I don't want the heartache, and I don't like walking through trials. But what I do long for is a strong sense of purpose and oneness with Christ. I want the growth and wisdom and beauty and peace and joy that come from suffering well for and with Christ.

I'm finally starting to accept that Christ makes Himself known to me when things are uncomfortable, messy, frustrating, chaotic, and painful. I am learning to live in the ebb and flow of trials while maintaining the joy I knew was there all along.

Defined by God

The English clergyman William Jenkyn is credited with saying, "As the wicked are hurt by the best things, so the godly are bettered by the worst." I heard this quote on a podcast, and something in me cringed. I didn't want to go through the worst things anymore. The resentment and bitterness from the trauma I've faced were slowly creeping back in.

But in that moment, I was reminded of the disciples. Each of the disciples faced extremely rough trials, including suffering and death, yet they knew without a doubt they were not forgotten or forsaken by Jesus. Although accounts vary, historians believe the following is true:[4]

> Paul was beheaded.
> Peter was crucified upside down.
> Andrew was crucified.
> Thomas died when soldiers pierced him with spears.
> Philip was put to death cruelly.

Matthew was likely stabbed to death.

Bartholomew was a martyr for Christ.

James (son of Alphaeus) was stoned and then clubbed to death.

Simon the Zealot was killed when he refused to sacrifice to a false god.

Matthias was burned to death.

Judas (son of James) was a martyr for Christ.

James (son of Zebedee) was killed by the sword.

John was exiled.

Despite their tragic ends, these men were faithful to God's call and carried the good news of the gospel throughout the regions of Syria, Asia Minor, Persia, North Africa, and beyond. I thought to myself, *Why in the world do I think I deserve a great and pain-free life as a Christian?* I still have so much to learn about suffering and living a joy-filled life for Christ. While being crucified or burned to death because of our allegiance to Christ is an unlikely event in modern America, I was convicted. I should be sharing more about the miracles Christ has done in my life instead of the pain He's allowed. I am not defined by the tragedy I've walked through but by who God says I am. And God's love is always unchanging, even when our circumstances change.

As John 16:33 says, "I have told you these things, so that in me you may have peace. In this world you will have trouble. But take heart! I have overcome the world" (NIV).

I know how difficult it can be to have hope when your world has been turned upside down. I know how painful it is to remain content while trying to move forward. I know how dark life can get and how much evil can surround us. But remember how far God has brought you already and how this life, while beautiful and crazy and hard, is not the end. Our glorious hope and prized possession is Christ and Him alone. We can allow God to use our trials for His glory. As godly women, let's:

- be grounded in the Word
- believe the truth about our loving God
- forgive quickly and walk in grace
- serve those around us, not missing an opportunity
- fix our eyes on Jesus
- take responsibility for our time, words, actions, faith, and relationships while actively pursuing Jesus
- count our blessings instead of complaining
- relinquish control and allow God's plans to prevail
- be confident in who God made us to be, avoiding comparison at all costs
- take the time to reflect on all that God is teaching us, not rushing through pain
- fight to see the good that God is doing in the midst of our pain

We were created for a reason, and that is to point others to Christ and become more like Him. Through trials and tribulations, we will understand the character of God better. Through pain and persecution, we will experience oneness with Christ. Through suffering and difficulties, we will learn that whatever the cost, serving God is always worth it.

We have decisions to make:

> Will we allow God to use our pain for His good? Or will we hide behind our insecurities and hold on to fear?
>
> Will we release control and let Him make something beautiful out of a mess? Or will we try to save and protect ourselves?
>
> Will we humble ourselves enough to recognize He is sovereign? Or will we make life about ourselves and remain stuck in the muck?
>
> Will we stand on the truth of the gospel? Or will we cower at the first trial?

My prayer is that we choose wisely, friends. What we do now will make a huge difference when we're standing before a just God at the gates of heaven.

I am not defined by the tragedy I've walked through but instead by who God says I am.

Jesus said, "As for everyone who comes to me and hears my words and puts them into practice, I will show you what they are like. They are like a man building a house, who dug down deep and laid the foundation on rock. When a flood came, the torrent struck that house but could not shake it, because it was well built" (Luke 6:47–48 NIV).

God is serious about His commands, and He means what He says. When He promised to be with us and for us and love us and help us through, He meant it. We need to believe that with every fiber of our beings and *live* like we believe that. You can trust the living God as your ever-present help in time of need, providing strength and lasting joy.

A Final Word

Thank you for allowing me to share my journey of facing pain and the process of fighting for joy in all circumstances. While I failed at times, doubted, tried to protect myself, and didn't trust, I see how God sustained me through it all. I hope you can see God's loving hand in your life, regardless of the suffering you have experienced. In spite of much pain that has come my way, I am grateful. Not because I loved walking through it all, but because I see what God *did* through it all. Although I once felt worthless, I'm married to an incredible godly man. Despite fighting cancer, I was able to get pregnant again and have a beautiful baby girl. As of today, I am healthy with no sign of disease, have four precious kids, and finally know my worth in Christ. Does this mean my life is only going to be great from here on out? No. I understand that life is filled with heartache but that life is also but a breath compared to eternity.

Today, I am grateful. Today, I will focus on what God has carried me through and how He has brought purpose into my life through suffering. Today, I will forgive where necessary, focus on my own purpose, and release control. Today, I will search for the beauty and joy around me and count my blessings instead of wishing hard years away. Today, I will study God's Word so I can stand firm in my faith.

Tomorrow, I will start over again. You can too. Let's focus on Jesus, the only One who can save, heal, restore, redeem, and change the trajectory of our lives. He is our joy.

Closing Prayer

Lord, I am so humbled and grateful that You have walked with me through every challenge, trial, and devastation. I know that the only reason I am still here today is because You're not done with me yet. I desire to partner with You and be used by You to bring You glory. Give me the strength and endurance to stand strong in the face of trials, and provide rest and stillness when I'm still learning to heal. Turn my failures and hardship into a heart attitude that reflects You and only You. Fill me with the Spirit today as I become the person You made me to be: victorious, valued, and a reflection of You to this world.

Thank You for the precious gift of life and relationship with You because of the death of Your Son on the cross. I choose to trust You with my life. Change me and mold me into a woman of strength who doesn't cower at the first sign of trials. I pray for the discipline and the obedience to truly know who You are as I study the Word. I need You and I give You my life, for You are worth it all. I believe that You were sacrificed in my place, and I commit my life to You today. I repent of my sins and ask that You would be made known in my life. I pray that my pain would be used for Your purpose and that You would restore to me the joy that comes only from You. My life is Yours. I love You, Jesus. In Your name I pray, amen.

If you made the decision to submit to Christ and follow Him today through the preceding prayer, this is just the beginning of your story. I encourage you to connect with your local church so you can receive support and prayer from other Christians in your community. Life is more than hard sometimes, but there is much joy! You were bought with a price, you are highly valued, and you are deeply loved. I can't wait to see what God does in and through you.

reflections

_____
_____
_____
_____
_____
_____
_____
_____
_____
_____
_____
_____
_____
_____
_____
_____
_____
_____
_____
_____
_____
_____
_____
_____
_____

acknowledgments

Andrew: Thank you for being the one constant in my life, the shoulder I sob on, ever-listening ears, an extra set of eyes on this book, for speaking truth even when I don't want to hear it, for being my better half, and for always pushing me to Jesus. You're the best thing that has ever happened to me.

Jacobsmeyer kids: Thank you for snuggling with me while I write, for being excited for me even though you might not fully understand, and for loving me even when I was extra exhausted while writing. I love you, my Fab Four!

Mom: Thank you for seeing the best in me even when I couldn't and for all your prayers that have sustained me through the seasons of my life.

Grandma and Grandpa: Thank you for the constant love, support, and wisdom you've shown me since the day I was born. I'm so blessed to have you both in my life.

All my sweet friends: Thank you for standing by my side through the hardest seasons of my life, for celebrating with me during the best times, and for all your grace and encouragement over the years (and decades).

Ingrid: You saw something in me despite my brokenness and cared enough to believe in me. Thank you for your patience and hard work and for being in my corner. I couldn't have done this without you.

DCC team—Stephanie, Susan, Annette, Judy, Katie, James: Thank you for all the time you poured into my message, for your talent, and for your kindness.

notes

Introduction: is this as good as life gets?

1. J. I. Packer, *Knowing God* (Downers Grove, IL: IVP Books, 1993), 34.

Chapter 1: be grounded in the word

1. Online Etymology Dictionary, s.v. "disciple," 2022, www.etymonline.com/word/disciple.

2. Thomas Guthrie, *The Way to Life: Sermons by Thomas Guthrie* (New York: Robert Carter & Brothers, 1863), 91.

Chapter 2: believe the truth about God

1. G. Campbell Morgan, quoted in David Guzik, "John 11—Jesus Raises Lazarus from the Dead," Enduring Word, 2018, https://enduringword.com/bible-commentary/john-11.

Chapter 3: choose forgiveness

1. Lysa TerKeurst, *Forgiving What You Can't Forget: Discover How to Move On, Make Peace with Painful Memories, and Create a Life That's Beautiful Again* (Nashville, TN: Nelson Books, 2020), 111.

Chapter 5: adjust your perspective

1. C. S. Lewis, letter to Arthur Greeves, December 20, 1943, in *The Collected Letters of C. S. Lewis,* ed. Walter Hooper, vol. 2, *Books, Broadcasts, and the War* (San Francisco: HarperSanFrancisco, 2004), 595.

Chapter 7: take responsibility

1. John Bunyan, *The Pilgrim's Progress: A Readable Modern-Day Version of John Bunyan's "Pilgrim's Progress,"* ed. Alan Vermilye (Mount Juliet, TN: Brown Chair Books, 2020), 121.

2. Dictionary.com, s.v. "responsible," 2022, www.dictionary.com/browse /responsible.

3. Bunyan, *The Pilgrim's Progress*, 63.

Chapter 8: stop complaining

1. "How Do Thoughts and Emotions Affect Health?," University of Minnesota, accessed July 12, 2021, www.takingcharge.csh.umn.edu/how-do-thoughts-and -emotions-affect-health#:~:text=Negative%20attitudes%20and%20feelings%20 of,and%20damages%20the%20immune%20system.

Conclusion: the purpose in the pain

1. C. S. Lewis, *Mere Christianity* (New York: HarperOne, 2001), 196–97.

2. Lewis, *Mere Christianity*, 141.

3. Nancy R. Pearcey, *Love Thy Body: Answering Hard Questions about Life and Sexuality* (Grand Rapids, MI: Baker Books, 2018), 40.

4. Ken Curtis, "Whatever Happened to the Twelve Apostles?," Christianity.com, April 28, 2010, www.christianity.com/church/church-history/timeline/1-300 /whatever-happened-to-the-twelve-apostles-11629558.html.

bible credits

about the author

Nicole Jacobsmeyer is a homemaker, chocolate chip cookie lover, entrepreneur, and writer. She believes that no matter what trials you're going through or how difficult your past was, Jesus can help you overcome it to walk in victory. She and her husband have four precious kiddos and reside in North Carolina. Nicole loves hearing from you, so follow her on Instagram @nicole.jacobsmeyer or head on over to her website at www.nicolejacobsmeyer.com.